Beginner to Climbing Mt Everest – A Practical Guide and Tips

Author: Michael Tomordy

CONTENTS PAGE

1. Forward 5

2. Preface - Whom is this Guide written for? 7

3. Caveats 8

4. About the Author 10

5. Can I Summit Mt Everest? 11

6. What does it take to Summit Mt Everest? 14

7. How to choose an Expedition Company? 19

8. Preparation – proper preparation prevents poor performance 24

9. Physical Training – Train Harder to climb Easier 38

10. Technical Training - Alpine 43

11. Training your Mind and Brain – hand-in-hand with the Body 49

12. Your fellow Climbers – the "team dynamic" 53

13. Personal Risk Management - The Risks and How to reduce 55

14. Timeline Overview – 2 months 63

15. The Route – beyond Base Camp to the Summit and Return 71

16. The End – the "Job is done" 97

Acknowledgements 98

Disclaimer 98

View from Mt Pumori C1 looking towards Lhotse Face and swirling clouds and winds above the Lhotse Summit. Everst shoulder to the left.

"We are mere mortals, specks of dust in the wind"

1. Forward – By Dan Mazur

I climbed Baruntse and did the Everest Camp 3 Training Climb with Michael Tomordy. He and I have kept in touch over the years. I have visited with his lovely family on several occasions. I would like to say they are my friends.

I appreciate Michael's frankness, politeness, caution, relaxed but
intelligent and perceptive style, his fitness, sense of humour, and
go-for-it, lets get the job done attitude. I feel honoured to have knownMichael for a fairly long time, and have enjoyed watching him develop his robust outlook on life.

This book, in many ways, expresses where Michael is now, an accomplished Everest Summiter, who has worked very hard to be where he is now. However,when I first met Michael so many years ago, he was just beginning his pursuit of the high peaks, and I like to think of this book as a tale of what he has learned along the way in his journey through life

This book should be required reading for not only those who are considering going to Everest, but also for people who are fascinated to learn what makes mountain climber "tick". I will certainly recommend this guidebook to anyone I meet who is thinking of climbing the "Big One".

I really like how Michael has broken down the preparation for and the process of climbing Everest into clear steps, from the concrete physical things, to more philosophical considerations.

He has written one of the best descriptions I have read about the mental part of climbing Everest, which is often ignored. I like Michael's ability to articulate how he not only focuses on his goal and the task at hand, but also how he deals with unexpected challenges and the potential disappointment of things not working out in the way he would have wanted. Important lessons indeed, as well as an ethos for living in this world.

His physical training section is good. I am going to use it in my own work and recommend that my own climbing team members follow his suggested training regimens.

I like the gear review section, it realistically deals with each piece of
kit and explains the pros and cons. There are lots of good pointers and hints about gear here.

I like the way he weaves in respect for the mountain environment and the people who live and work there. His section on how to choose a company is extensive and very well thought out.

He has a very good section on how to prepare your life affairs for an
Everest climb. I never thought about addressing the issue in such a way, a very pragmatic and respectful approach.

I like Michael's slow and steady methodical approach to gaining experience by taking climbing courses and ascending smaller mountains first. The author is a patient man, and his patience has payed off with success at the highest altitude.

Overall, I love the humility in the Author's tone of voice. For example,take his "Constant Beginner Mindset". Michael is an observant respectfulperson who is aware that taking a cautious and go-slow approach can yield big results when the time is right.

This is one of the big lessons Michael teaches us in this book, walk softly,be humble but observant, watching for signs all around you, and inside yourself, and then when the time is right, be physically fit and mentally prepared to go for it. Get to the top and come down safely. Keep your respect for others and the environment around us. Throughout the entire book, Michael has maintained his positive outlook on life and sense of humour. A good example for all of us to follow, no matter how large or small the challenge, and a wonderful book that we can learn from, and incorporate into our high mountain climbs and everyday life.

About Dan Mazur
Dan Mazur is an active mountain climber, expedition leader and organizer who also volunteers his time giving back to mountain communities with health care, education, environmental and cultural preservation. Not only has Dan climbed 8 of our world's 8000 metre / 26,000 foot high peaks, but he has also been involved in rescues of fellow climbers from high altitudes. For his services to mountaineering, to mountain peoples and environments, Mazur has been selected to receive the Sir Edmund Hillary Mountain Legacy Medal on December 11, 2018 (International Mountain Day), in Pokhara, Nepal.

Michael and Dan In Morraine near BC - Comms.

2. Preface - Whom is this Guide written for?

Well Done, you are reading this book! You have likely made an important and serious decision or about too. I congratulate you and wish you the very best of British Luck!

I wrote this simple practical guide or "tip book" following my successful Summit on 0600 hours 23 May 2018 and realized that there was much I learnt on the mountain, prior expeditions and similar challenges, that could help others achieve their Goal, and more importantly that I had not been told, read in books, watched in documentaries or exaggerated in the movies! This practical guide is primarily written for the "Amateur" or beginner Mountaineer, but much of its content equally applies to those whom are more experienced. I am sorry if you don't like the word Amateur, you can use whatever word makes you feel "less small or embarrassed", a Novice, a Beginner, a Highly Motivated (Dead) Person. This is the first tip and test for you in the guide, learn to "eat humble pie". The Mountain doesn't care who you are, what you have done, whom you Think you are, why you are attempting the Summit. That's all in your human psychology, your mind.

This Guide is written to provide practical guidance and tips to hopefully make your experience better and help you achieve whatever your goal is, whether Mt Everest Summit or "your Everest". It is intended to be complementary to your Expedition Company and Leaders advice, both pre-arrival and on the mountain.

It is not written in an emotional style, unlike the majority of the books that have Mt Everest in the title or intended to dramatize the experience, therefore its perhaps a bit "dry" in places.

It is intended to be concise and for you to read before and during your Expedition. Equally, I cannot hope or intend to cover 100% of the totality of an Expedition to Mt Everest, else this Guide would become an Encyclopaedia - there are various reference books you can buy on Motivation, Fitness and Mountaineering. I am not intentionally advertising any products, services or companies (and not sponsored by any company). It is certainly not intended to chronical my personal journey to the Summit, although will express my particular observations and feelings, in the context of learning points for yourselves.

This is the first time I have written any book or Guide. I have no Sports Science or Sports Psychology background. I am not a Personal Trainer, Motivational Speaker, work in a Tour Company or Sponsored by anyone, rather an Engineer with a day job. Some aspects of this Guide will touch on what some may say is Sports Science, Sports Psychology and so forth, certainly yes, but based on my personal experience in the context of Mt Everest.

This Guide will "unpack" some of these ideas and more together with what does it actually mean in real practical terms of Mt Everest. I am going to be expressing how I felt at different times in terms of "when the going got tough", what mental, physical techniques and practical measures did I apply.

Finally I also believe many of the items covered in this practical guide can equally be applied to other similar rigorous challenges. I wish you success and safe return from "Your Everest", whatever it might be.

Thank you
Michael Tomordy. michaeltomordy@hotmail.com

3. CAVEATS

Climbing Mt Everest is inherently dangerous, there are risks. Mt Everest and other similar Mountains are not like other endurance sports, like multi-day running, cycling, swimming. There is a clear increased risk of injury, serious medical condition or death on Mt Everest. It is Your Choice and only you are Responsible for the choices and decisions you make, both signing-up and going on the Expedition. I am not trying to encourage you, it is your choice, this book is primarily written as Practical Guide and Tips for once you have made that Commitment to sign-up.

Safety should be your primary consideration and that of your Expedition Company, although there is a fine line between Safety and Risk, Bravery and Stupidity when it comes to Mountaineering. However there are no guarantees and total safety is simply impossible to achieve, there are risks that you cannot manage. You need to accept this if you are to attempt Mt Everest.

As a minimum, follow what your Expedition Company and Medically trained professionals advise you - the Criteria, Pre-Arrival Requirements, Training, Experience, Expertise and Personal Gear List your Expedition provides - don't be arrogant, stupid and ignore it – you are paying them for their expertise. Listen and follow the advice of your Expedition Leadership, including Leaders, Sherpas, Base-Camp Staff and HQ Staff.

Medical advice and Medicines. You should seek medical advice from a medically trained professional, both pre-arrival and during the expedition if you are suffering from any symptoms, including in the use of medicines, especially for Acute Mountain Sickness (AMS) type symptoms.

Base Camp 2014 post Avalanche Sherpa gathering

Near Namche, trekking to BC. Plume off the Summit Mt Everest on the left.

4. ABOUT THE AUTHOR

I am 47 years old and born in North London, England. I have an Electronic Engineering Degree and completed a Short Service Limited Commission in the British Army (Royal Signals). I also joined the 10th Battalion The Parachute Regiment.

I moved to Hong Kong in 1998, just when Hong Kong was "handed-back" from the British to China and became a Special Autonomous Region. I worked for a large Engineering Consultant until 2012 when I started my own business, www-engage-asia-Ltd, providing Technical Risk and Technology Consulting Services.

I have a family, a typically small apartment in Hong Kong and a mortgage. I enjoy the countryside and hiking in Hong Kong. I am off above average fitness for my age, certainly not an Iron Man or engaged in similar activities.

I started high-altitude Mountaineering in later years, in my late thirties, and very limited prior Rock Climbing type experience. A friend suggested a 7,500m Mountain called Mt Mustagata in the Pamirs, off the Silk Road. I thought, he must be joking, why do I want to climb a 7500m as my first high altitude mountain? Alternatively, I could still be watching the documentaries and movies from the comfort of my arm-chair and therefore never summitted Mt Everest. It's about bringing what's in the background of your thoughts to the foreground. It's about making that decision to take that first positive first step, "jumping out of the plane", taking a risk and surprising yourself. I was successful at Mt Mustagata and have since been on trips long and short around the world, including the European Alps, Andes, Caucasus, Sichuan, Himalaya (Tibet and Nepal), Pamirs and last but not least winter climbing in Scotland. I am a novice, an amateur, I consider myself a "constant beginner". I would also say that a large number of my Expeditions have resulted in Failure to Summit, but the Summit is only one point on the mountain, part of the journey, part of the learning experience and I have never been put off returning.

In 2014 I joined a Training Climb to Camp 3 Mt Everest Nepal which was ended prematurely by an Avalanche in the Ice Fall that tragically killed 16 Sherpas. At times Mountaineering is also about being Lucky, a bit like "Russian Roulette" and we watched the rescue and recovery of bodies from Base Camp. I tried the same Training Climb expedition to Camp 3 in 2017 and was successful. In October 2017, 6 months after returning, I decided to attempt the Summit. I cannot say its been my "life's ambition", my decision making was rationale and objective, and I felt "zen-calm" (mostly!) both prior and during the Expedition. I felt confident I was ready to try for the Summit, born from experience the previous year, but equally I was not arrogant. I summited Mt Everest Nepal side on 23 May 2018 0600 hours, the day after the Buddha's Birthday, this was my first attempt going for the Summit.

5. CAN I SUMMIT MT EVEREST?

Yes, you can, if you really want it and provided you:
1. put in the right type and quantity of **Training**,
2. gain relevant **Experience** and
3. have the right **Mind-set** and be Positive.

Be realistic about your goal and whether you can achieve it within the timeframe you have set or adjust accordingly and come back next year – the Mountain will still be there, but you may not ,if you take too big a risk and are ill prepared.

The right training and the right experience is a critically important point to note. There are many people who have lots of experience on Mountains, yet their experience may be bad, not relevant or not the right experience for Mt Everest. This equally applies to Physical Fitness. You may be a super-fit athlete but not mountain-fit – there is a difference.

You first need to make that fundamental decision that you want to sign-up and attempt Mt Everest. You have those doubts, concerns, questions in your mind. Can I really make the Summit? Am I fit enough? Do I have the Skills? Will I die? Equally, the flip-side is that there are unintended Conseqences if you decide not to attempt the Summit – you may have regrets for the rest of your life, and be frequently reminded given the "fame" of Mt Everest and the media coverage. These same consequences equally apply if you failed or gave-up during your Expedition. It comes down to **How badly do you want it?**

Most people have not faced their own mortality and what seems a very small probability of their life ending. It is difficult to practically think about death, perhaps except thru quiet Contemplation before signing-up. Death can happen to anyone whether a beginner or world-class mountaineer. The possibility may make you appreciate your life and mortality more, but hopefully not put you off – it is the inherent risk with Mountaineering. The Fear of death may stop you from making the most critical decision – to Sign-up for Mt Everest Expedition. The reality is that you summit to understand the possibility, put it to one side and sign-up.

All of these risks, concerns, and doubts you can actually work to mitigate or reduce, which will improve your chances and change the odds in your favour. This I will explain, but ultimately you need to make the decision to "jump out of the plane" (and hope the parachute opens). You may try to take short-cuts such as not putting in the time, or getting the right mountain experience and training. You may Summit but the risks and probabilities of failure are greater - don't fool yourself, you may have just been lucky.

I am a strong believer that the Mind, the Brain in conjunction with the Body can enable Success, almost more so then your Physical Strength and Technical Skill. There is a two-way interface between the Body and Brain, with the Brain being the Command, Control and Communication center for the Body, ultimately its your mind and brain that is making your decisions so you should spend time training your brain. As we know the reality is that most of the time people allocate for training is spent on Physical Fitness or Technical Skills and very little of training our Mind, getting that positive mind-set.

The Physical and Technical Training is the relatively "easy" part, which is about time (and secondly money) provided you have the above 3 qualities. In my view it is unlikely to be a lack of Fitness or Technical Skills that is the reason you don't achieve your Goal, rather one

or more of the above failing you. Understand this point very clearly, in my opinion you cannot Summit Mt Everest purely in the Belief that you have the determination to make it, you need the base-line, the internal reservoir of Physical Fitness/Endurance/Resilience and appropriate level of the right Technical Skills and the right Mountain Experience. Only then can you face what the Mountain has to throw at you. It would be delusional to think otherwise. On my Training Climb to Camp 3, there was someone going for the Summit, who had only limited Alpine Experience in the European Alps. This person did not want
to do the full acclimatisation hikes and was convinced by their Determination alone, based upon their hard-core Military background. They didn't make it past Base Camp. You may not have all these Qualities but if you are good with two out of three then hopefully you can make it.

Finally, in fact, it is relatively "easy" to Summit Mt Everest, Just don't give up! That sounds too simple, frivolous, but think about those simple, few words - Just dont give up!. This Resilience and ability to keep going thru adversity, is one of the most fundamental quality that you will need to develop and quality you will need to possess, and which you can develop over time, including through the "school of hard knocks". When you want to Quit it is, in fact, a failure of your Will-Power. You have decided its "too hard" and you will make various excuses for yourself to justify your decision to quit and what you tell others. You need to practice on other mountains situations when it got "too hard" and you continued. You will face many times when you are Suffering, you are Scared, you have Doubts, you may want to Quit and see others Quitting, well that's your choice. Now, I should also caveat the statement by saying, if you have for example Altitude Sickness, a broken ankle, terrible weather then those are probably acceptable reasons to undertake a rear-guard action, re-group, but you may not need to Quit completely either. Come back to fight another day, on this Expedition or future, it's not necessarily over, don't see it in finite terms of total Failure, keep your head up and think positively that simply re-grouping.

In this Guide, I will talk about the Physical, the Mental, the Technical Training and the Practical matters. I am going to avoid becoming too philosophical and "sports psychology" on you since there are far more qualified persons - remember this is a Practical Guide with tips, rather than a large Volume on Sports Science or Psychology

What is the best Age to attempt Summit?
There is no fixed best-age to climb and there would seem no clear correlation between Age and Summit success, however, the majority seem to be in the 30-45 age range, with some both younger and older. On our Expedition, we had 24, 44, 47, 51, 53 and 60 year olds (the later for Lhotse). Unfortunately, the 24 year old did not Summit yet the others did.
These are generalizations, but based on my observations:
- Younger people are generally faster and recover more quickly. They have the energy of youth, but perhaps naivety, lack experience and have less understanding of risk. They don't have responsibilities either.
- Older people will be more prone to injury, aches, and pains. Their Recovery time will take longer. However, it could be said that physical and mental endurance/resilience combined with experience/expertise and maturity are the benefits of age. Older people are generally more cautious but may have more will-power.

Can you Summit without any Mountaineering experience and "never used" personal Equipment?
Yes, you can, but understand the Risks to both yourself and others are considerably greater and the probability of failure is greater – I would not recommend it. By "others" I am referring to your team-mates, including Team Leaders and Sherpas and do think about the consequences for them also – you may equally jeopardise the entire team goal by your selfishness. In the context of Mt Everest, failure includes Injury, serious medical problems or even death.

Whilst we all need to start somewhere, I could not recommend Mt Everest as your first Mountain or first serious high-altitude mountain. You should ask yourself Why do this? Is it worth the Risk? You have more time to get better prepared, the mountain will still be there next year, as it has been for 60 million years, so reduce the risk and improve your chances of success. Take a step back and think rationally.

How Physically Fit do I need to be?
You need to have a reasonably good level of Fitness but you do not need to be super-fit. You don't necessarily need to be able to do an Iron Man or similar. In fact being super-fit is not likely to help you any more then less fit team member. Your training time 6 months prior to departure is finite. The time spent becoming super-fit may be better balanced by for example, doing Technical Alpine Training. If you are super-fit, then spend time on getting mountain-fit and your technical training.

6. WHAT DOES IT TAKE TO SUMMIT MT EVEREST?

There is no 100% guarantee you will make it, there is the unknown and plenty of variables, many out of your direct control. You need a mindset that will allow you to take a risk and to boldly go into the unknown, to a very hostile place, far outside of your comfort zone. Stand tall, embrace it., step-forward one step at a time – thats all that it takes, one step at a time.

What fundamental personal qualities to you need to have?
1. First, **Believe** that you can make it
2. Have the **Determination**, the mental Resilience and Toughness
3. Have the **Heart** - the passion, the drive, the desire

BELIEF
in Yourself that You will make it

Summit Success
Its in your Head and Heart

DETERMINATION
Mental Resilience to keep going

PASSION
in your Heart How badly do you want it

Arguably more importantly then the Physical and Technical Training, which should be your base-line training minimum requirements, is your **Positive Mind-set**.

It is very important that your mind is not "taken by the dark-side" and thinking about fear, all that can go wrong and even worse. You will have read about the Ice Fall and the Lhotse Face. I can assure you that once you cross these hurdles you will look back and think "maybe it wasnt as bad as I thought it would be".

Some of the following points to note:

Belief and Confidence – believe in yourself Fundamentally, It's whether you Believe its possible to Summit and what's in your Heart. In the end, it's not whether you have all the best and most expensive mountaineering personal equipment and clothing, whether you have paid USD100,000 and two Sherpas, whether you have Summitted many other mountains and have the best technical skills or physical fitness in the group - its what's in your Head and Heart that counts.

<u>I don't think one can simply say "I Believe I can make it" without something behind it, which would otherwise be delusional.</u> This confidence should be backed up by evidence, facts to give you that belief or confidence i.e. the right training and the right experience. For myself I went on a Training Climb to Camp 3 the year before, 2017, which was successful. This gave me a good understanding, confidence and a real Belief that I could attempt the Summit. When I decided 6 months before departure in April that I would sign-up for the Summit, I felt very zen-calm, I was not apprehensive, I had great belief that I could make the Summit. This doesn't mean I was arrogant or complacent about the challenge ahead, rather the complete opposite because I was well aware of the route already - it's about being realistic, objective and honest. Confidence from Skill and to gain Skills we need Experience.

Constant Beginner approach. See yourself as a "constant beginner". With this mindset, you will be humble (not arrogant), cautious (which also doesn't mean overly slow), not be complacent and focus on getting the basics right. Be open to advice from others and listen to learn from them.

Just Don't Give Up! When you are going up the Lhotse Face it may be like a "See-Saw" in your mind – "forces of positivity" telling you to keep going and overwhelming darkness telling you to Quit, dragging you down, because you are suffering, maybe scared and heart and lungs are bursting. You need to find that 1% to keep going. Equally, Failure or effectively turning around is your decision ultimately. If you are comfortable with the decision then you should have no regrets about this and be calm. On a big Mountain it is not uncommon to fail.

When you are at the point of quitting, stop and remind yourself "Why did you want to come here originally?". Lift your head up and continue.

When you are at the point of quitting, ask yourself this practical question, "I have come this far, will I ever come back here in the future or just have regrets (there are consequences...)?" You have come this far, invested considerable time and money, lift your head up and continue.

When you are at your lowest point, head down, look inside yourself and show the mountain whom you are, find it, you can do it, stand tall and Rise to the Challenge.

At certain points you will be faced with situations, perhaps bad weather, it will become a personal critical decision-making point, to retreat or to continue. Remember everyone is faced with the same decision, some retreat whilst other go onwards, it's in your mind how you perceive the risk and level of suffering. At this most critical failure/success point you need to step up to the task, else your expedition may be over. In the end, its how do you feel in yourself, are you content with your decision or will you have regrets. Each person has a different risk appetite, abilities and personal goals, so dont necessarily compare or judge yourself based on others.

Do not be Complacent. You will get lazy, distracted and fed-up of the repetition, for example, clipping in and out of the line. It's when you enter a mental comfort-zone, forget to do the basics, become complacent and less disciplined that accidents are more likely to happen. These accidents can have serious consequences.

Do the simple things, do them well, always. Remember the Basics. Most of the time you will need your basic mountaineering skills and repeat these on a constant basis. Therefore practice the basics many times, rather than the full spectrum of technical climbing and experience that is not relevant and specific for Mt Everest. Focus and Practice.

As Hong Kong native Bruce Lee said "I fear not the man who has practiced 10000 kicks once, but I fear the man who has practiced one kick 10000 times."

Attention to detail. For example, when you put your crampons on, check them, and again. Is the strap pulled tight? When you put your harness on, check the buckle and straps are correct, all clicked-in and pulled tight, above your hips, in case you fall off the ladder. Ask your Sherpa or buddy to check you.

Luck. Luck helps with success and you can improve your luck. It's often better to be Lucky than relying on being Good. It doesn't matter who you are, you may be lucky or unlucky, and it sometimes feels a bit like Russian Roulette, whether a rock hits you or you fall in a crevasse. What's more important is how you manage bad luck. You may be unlucky and get an illness, suffer from insomnia or fall in a crevasse. You may feel this is not fair, you may have your "head in your hands", "Why isn't anyone else suffering like me?" Well, Deal with it. The mountain isn't discriminating against you personally and choosing who is going to be lucky or not. Lift your head up and fight hard thru it - the next day will be better. Stand tall, look up to the Summit, and get inspiration and walk-on!

Be Humble, have Humility and don't be Arrogant. Whomever you are back home, leave it behind. Dont be the "tough guy", rather have some humility. Remember, the Mountain was formed 60 miilion years ago and you will be on this Planet for maybe 80 years (maybe less, depending on how the Expedition goes) and you will be on Everest for 2 months only. You are a mere mortal, a speck of dust in the wind.

An Open-Mind. Rather than a closed-mind or an arrogance that you are a "skilled mountaineer" or not concerned about the risks since you have read that Mt Everest is not the most technically difficult mountain, or paid top-dollar and have two personal Sherpas - have Humility. Be ready to accept information. You need a balance between Confidence, Humility and an Open-mind.

Respect. Respect the Mountain and all sections you move thru. Respect the Environment. Respect the local communities and all people you will meet on your expedition. Cultural awareness of Nepal, its peoples, customs, the way of life and the more practical matters about the food and the noisy streets, hawkers and traffic jams in Thamel. Respect and understand your fellow team members. Don't get angry, although there will be times when we are all tested, everyone will have highs and lows and experiencing different emotions at different times.

Rationale and Objective. You will find the Expedition to be a more or lesser an emotional experience. Emotions are important but you need to control and manage them also. You need to be very calm, rational and objective in your personal Decision Making, which can be difficult in a stress situation, when your emotional side of your brain is taking over. Be cognisent of this and manage your emotions.

Optimistic and pragmatic at the same time. Be realistic about the situation and yourself. Yes, have a positive outlook despite however bad the situation or weather looks, but don't have your head in the sand, in denial about the realities.

Listen to your Body and how you are feeling. You need to make adjustments to your day, to your expedition accordingly. Your body and mind is a system with sensory inputs and outputs. You wouldn't drive a car when the wheels are falling off or no petrol in the tank.

Learn to Suffer. You are going to suffer more or less on this Expedition. It may be the altitude, it may be an upset stomach. Practice suffering on other mountains. You need to practice mentally that you are going to suffer. This is one factor that may cause you to quit.

Being Selfish. This is a selfish sport and you are selfish, not distracted by others, focussed on the goal and focussed on your inner-self and self-confident, if you haven't realized by now. You are singularly driven, competitive, have an inner strength, block out the fear and suffering. Face this fact, embrace it, you will need it. You will be angry when others compromise your ability to succeed and your desire to drive on, upwards.

Single-Minded. I distinguish between being single-minded and focused on your goal, which is required, from being Selfish and specifically selfish towards your Team. You need to think that your actions may have consequences on others in your team, most likely negative, which should be avoided.

Decision Making is critical to all aspects of the Expedition and your personal safety. People make mistakes thru bad decision making, including and especially on the Summit Push, not wanting to turn-around, over-taken by emotion or altitude sickness, when logic and rationale reasoning would say they should Go Down. If you were to analyze the most serious accidents then very often it's down to poor decision making, by either the Climber, team-mates or both. Equally, listen and act on the advice from the professionals i.e. Leaders and Sherpas.

"Don't spit your dummy out". If you are "highly strung" emotional individual then Mt Everest is likely to severely test your ability to be calm and think rationally. Equally, it will impact negatively on the team dynamic and ultimately team chance of success. Be Zen-Calm, clear your mind, Relax but be Focussed and stay Switched-On. This will certainly be a "memorable" rather than perhaps "enjoyable" experience, and you should try to be calm, relax, be happy but at the same time be focused, particularly when moving

Yin and Yang. For example, on one-hand you need Drive and Determination to keep going but on the other-hand you need to know when Not to leave your Tent, when to turn-around, when the conditions are too bad, when you are suffering from Altitude symptoms

Zen. Find a balance. Try and be Open-minded and be Calm. There are many aspects of a Zen Buddism approach that may be applicable to Mt Everest, as I have introduced throughout this Guide.

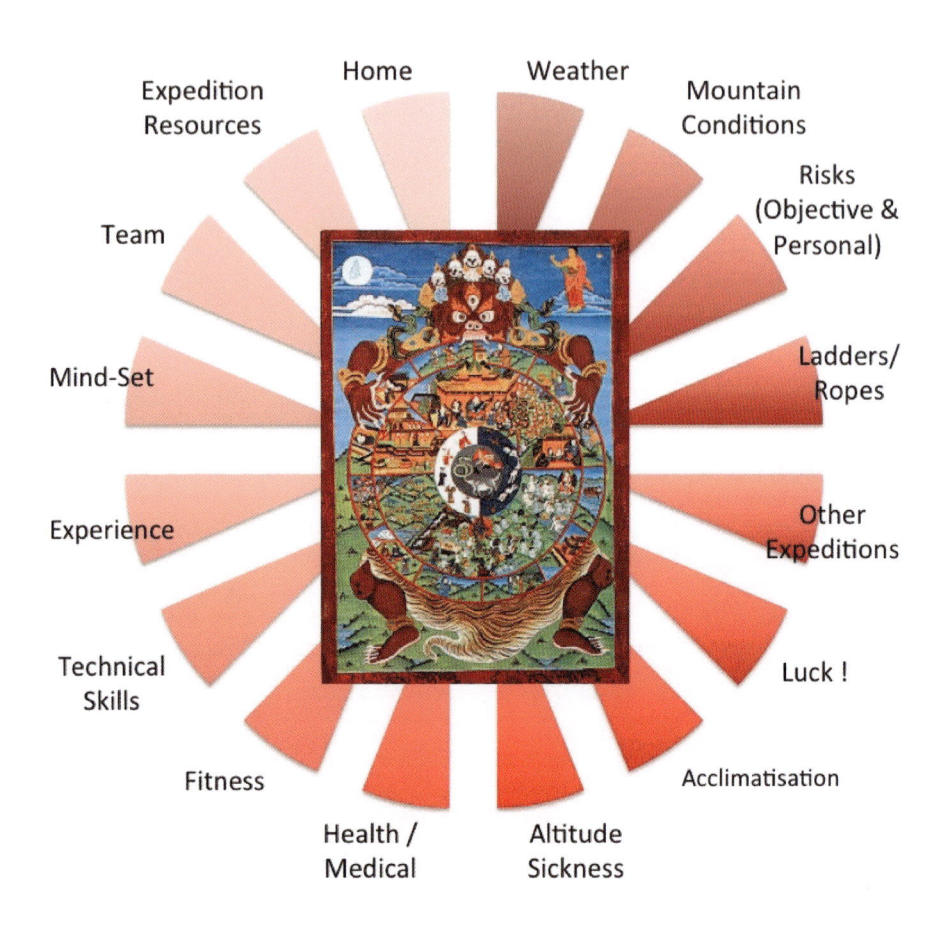

- Home
- Weather
- Mountain Conditions
- Risks (Objective & Personal)
- Ladders/Ropes
- Other Expeditions
- Luck !
- Acclimatisation
- Altitude Sickness
- Health / Medical
- Fitness
- Technical Skills
- Experience
- Mind-Set
- Team
- Expedition Resources

7. How to choose an Expedition Company?

There are many Expedition Companies, both International and Local to Nepal. Myself I have used the same company Summit Climb, https://www.summitclimb.com/ for all my major Expeditions, because I am comfortable with them - I know what I am getting. I know them, the Leaders, the Sherpas, their Style. It would surely make common-sense to consider doing the same, to use the same Company that you are familiar with on other Expeditions, for such a serious endeavor and thereby providing one less uncertainty, one less risk or doubt in your mind.

Some questions to consider:

- Style – some companies are very "gung-ho", regimented, disciplined, not-friendly, arrogant whilst others are the opposite to the point of being laid-back – what do you want?
- Flexibility - you are a paying customer. You should be able to make requests, rather than purely "dictated to" on all matters, whilst appreciating the seriousness of the endeavor ahead and need for safety. Equally, you may want decisions made for you and no flexibility! Understand very clearly, there are constraints including for your safety and it's not a matter of just doing what you want, which may equally put others at risk.
- Success/Failure Rates. Try to learn Why people were successful or otherwise from past expeditions.
- What's their approach to Risk and going down or not?
- Experience - How many Everest Summit Attempts and other High Altitude Mountains?
- Expertise - Leaders and Sherpas. How many Everest Summit Attempts and Summits for the leadership team specifically on Mt Everest? Other High Altitude Mountains? You may ask but in reality, it may be difficult to know the exact number and names of those whom will be on the Expedition or whether backup Sherpas if things go wrong, particularly at higher-camps and Summit Push.
- Resources – Kathmandu, Lukla Transport connections, Base Camp Resources, Porters in addition to the Moutain Leaders and Sherpas.
- How are Team Members selected? Are there enforced minimum standards or pre-cursors that team members must achieve before being signed-up? How rigorously are these minimum requirements validated and met? The team members and their experience or lack of may directly impact your chance of summit success.
- How many Members in Expedition? If there are a large number you will likely be split into teams. It could be argued that larger team results in more challenges on Expedition Leadership Resources, Leader(s) time shared amongst more people, logistics, and critical issues like Which team ascends first and so forth. The later will become critical during the Summit Week. You should ask How are teams selected, based on what criteroa and what team are you likely to be placed within?
- Base Camp Food - ask for the menus, and drill hard on this. Is there meat including chicken, steak, lamb chops and solid vegetables like potatoes or only "mystery meat"?
- Team Leadership - what is their Everest Leadership and other similar experience? How far up the Mountain will the Leader go? How far will the Second In Command (2IC) go up the Mountain? How will it be managed on Summit Push?

- Sherpas - their experience, how many, what ratio Sherpa/Member. How is your personal Sherpa selected?
- Load Carries – will the Sherpas carry your personal gear up/down the mountain beyond Base Camp? If so, how much weight and on what basis? Are there extra costs involved?
- Doctor - is there a Team Doctor or whom has the medical knowledge?
- High Altitude Drugs - will the Expedition distribute to team members or how to manage supply and administering, particularly on Summit Day? The reality is that it will be others who determine whether you have HAPE, HACE and need the drugs or to Descend.
- Expedition Duration - there is some variation depending on the Company, but typically 2 months
- Expedition Plan and Rotations - this is critical and you should check, particularly the rotations and will you be "forced" to do whatever rotations you are told.
- Will you potentially be allowed a "2nd attempt" at the Summit if you dont make it on the first night, from C4 (assuming all factors and sufficient resources) ?
- Cut-Off Timing and stopping Members who "don't meet the grade" – will your Expedition stop you from a Summit attempt if they don't think you are capable or ready (this is not necessarily a bad thing)?
- Oxygen. You need Oxygen, buy more then the minimum recommended. However the critical question is Can I buy more Oxygen once in Nepal or on the mountain or do I need to decide many months before starting the Expedition? Also, at What Cost?
- Local Knowledge, local Connections - this is important if things go wrong or the headaches of logistics, transport and duffle-bag transportation, especially down-valley
- Cost – I put this last deliberately, the price range will be similar for medium grade Company. But especially watch out for Hidden Extras e.g. extra Oxygen Bottles, Helicopters.

Flexibility.
1. There is going to be a lot happening and a lot of variables. Remember each person is different and what works for somebody else may not work for you. You may want more "hand holding" and decisions made for you vs. flexibility to make your own decision based on information and resources available to support your decision
2. What do I mean by Flexibility?
    a. It's Your Expedition.
    b. Will you be forced to go up/down from Base Camp on certain days/times or is there flexibility?
    c. Will you be forced to do a certain number of rotations with the team or can you do less or different acclimatization?
    d. Will you be required to, for example, do Lobuche East and 2 or 3 Rotations, sleeping at C3 ultimately or is there personal choice and flexibility?

Rotations - Acclimatisation
1. Rotations relate primarily to Acclimatisation, which is very critical to your success or otherwise, however there is no right or wrong answer, since very dependent on how you as individual feel. It is about your body's ability to Adapt to the altitude over a given period of time. The most important point is to listen to Your Body and how

You are feeling, not others. Ideally, you want the Flexibility to adjust your personal acclimatization programme (this depends on the Company also).
- a. Briefly, you will do training hikes as you approach Base Camp - do this diligently and don't think "I don't need to trek up that hill".
- b. Do I need to do Lobuche East? It seems one or two Companies advocate this. This depends on their acclimatisation strategy. The argument is to spend time up high, prior to arriving Mt Everest whch has the larger number of objective risks. There is a risk you exhaust yourself, especially if your Expedition Company combines with multiple Ice Fall rotations, and the objective risk is thereby increased.
- c. Do I need to do 2 or even 3 rotations to C3 or What is Enough? I don't think necessary but depends whether your Company is flexible or not. All Companies will make you go at least once to C3. The downside with multiple rotations is more time in the Ice Fall, above 6200m+ and therefore potentially increased risk and tiredness.
- d. Do I need to Sleep at C3 on final Acclimatization Rotation or "touch it" and return to C2? A traditional approach would suggest spending a night at C3. On our expedition, there was a debate and in the end, none of us stayed at C3, rather we touched it and returned to C2 in the same, long day. The argument for not staying at C3 is that it will drain you of energy spending a night at C3 and negatively impact your expedition. I am skeptical about this, you are going for the Summit after all. The previous year I did stay at C3 and believe it was beneficial, although this year I did not and I Summited. It's what you feel most comfortable about, particularly if you have limited 7000m+ experience, it may be more beneficial.
- e. Should I go beyond C3 further up the Lhotse Face in the morning after I sleep at C3 for acclimatization? This is tempting when you are at BC thinking ahead. It is generally not undertaken and most people want to descend after a night at C3!

Base Camp Setup.
1. What is provided in Base Camp, what are the Dining Tent Quality and practical things like tables, chairs, TV, Team WIFI, Team Solar, DVD, Lighting, carpet and so forth. A more robust and improved solution to personal power is a large Team Battery-Pack that is solar-charged.
2. What Group Medical provisions are there at BC, including Medicines, and for example, Gamow Bag

Base Camp Food.
1. What are the actual typical foods served for breakfast, lunch and dinner - "the menus"?
2. Is there Meat or Protein? This becomes critical if you don't get it because Carbo based food gets really boring!
3. Is there fresh fruit, vegetables, bread?

Cost.
1. Perhaps more importantly, then cost, are the soft-factors, since the cost of most medium-grade, typical Expeditions will be within USD 5-10,000 range. Today the average Cost is USD 40,000+.

2. Ask about the "Hidden Extras" and know the costs before you sign-up These may not be included in the base-Cost and you may want more e.g. especially Oxygen, Helicopters, Insurance, Hotels.
3. There are Private Guides at USD 100,000 and equally, low-cost Options at USD 15-20,000. I cannot recommend these two extremes.

Private Sherpa or Quarter Sherpa or no Sherpa ?
1. You are an Amateur, you need all the help you can get, no need for "heroics" (and you will realize quickly after Base Camp Why you need a Sherpa)
2. The Load carries are very important up the Mountain and you should clarify specifically your Personal Gear the amount of weight that your Sherpa or Group Sherpa will carry for you – every gram of weight you will try to get rid off as you realise how exhausted you will become.
3. When making your decision about Sherpa, you need to fully appreciate that most Everest Expeditions are not in fact "Guided", due to practical difficulties of doing this at 8000m and above. This means that the risk has increased since a Guide whom may be able to offer you more direct support on a lower altitude mountain is not likely to do so on Everest. The traditional Guide-Client relationship is not likely to be the case. A lot of responsibility is therefore on your shoulders and the people around you.
4. When you are on the mountain, if something goes wrong, it is the person next to you that is most likely to be most important and ideally that would be a Sherpa.
5. A Private Sherpa will provide more support to you and potentially carry more loads.
    a. They will, in theory, be close to you as you go between Camps.
    b. This is most important on the critical stages, particularly the final Summit Push, from C3 upwards.
    c. They will carry your additional personal gear between Camps.
    d. The cost is approximately USD 7000.
6. A Quarter Sherpa will primarily help with load carries, especially from BC upwards.
    a. This is typically 10kg load carries. In fact, 10kg is likely to be more than adequate in terms of loads.
    b. The cost is surprisingly about a quarter of a Private Sherpa, depending upon the Expedition Company!
7. If you can afford it, I would recommend a Private Sherpa, primarily for the comfort-factor on the critical stages. Apart from the Load carries, its to reduce Risk if things do go pear-shaped.
8. Let's be clear, without a Private Sherpa you are probably not "going to be left behind on the Summit", well hopefully not. There are other Sherpas and Team Members but you are not going to get as much "hand holding".
9. Equally, don't assume a Sherpa will be able to get you Up or Down, its about you ultimately. Whilst they appear super-human, compared to us, they can only do so much. Equally, they are not an "Insurance Policy".

References, "Interview". You should directly talk to the Company and past Members, especially the later, if you have not used the Company previously (which I would not recommend). Expedition Companies are commercial entities who want customers and therefore their Marketing will be worded very "positively", therefore talk directly to:
1. the Companies themselves, preferably operational leadership
2. others who have climbed Mt Everest with the Company. This is perhaps the most useful persons to ask questions too.
3. Ideally, the proposed Leaders, if they are identified?

Ideally, you want to use a Company and Staff that can get you out of a difficult situation. That is difficult to know, expect thru talking to them and others.

Ultimately, it will be How Comfortable do you feel with the different companies and individuals you are talking too, do they meet your personal preferences and address your concerns?

Finally, you have chosen the Company, they provide you a Home-Theatre and Lamb chops in a carpeted Dining Tent. Do not be deluded into a false sense of comfort, safety, and security or high confidence you will Summit because of the Expedition Company you have chosen – Mother Nature will become very hostile at some point in the next 2 months and it will come down to yourself personally and likely the Sherpa next to you, ultimately.

8. PREPARATION – PROPER PREPARATION PREVENTS POOR PERFORMANCE

Firstly, you should sign-up not less then 9 months before your trip, preferably 12 months, to give yourself adequate time to prepare.

Secondly, you may become overwhelmed with all the information that your Expedition Company throws at you, lots of questions you have in your mind, purchasing all the gear, planning, training, admin and so forth. Try to relax and another reason why more time will reduce your stress levels.

Finally, the best preparation cannot remove the Risks and there are no guarantees. Also, when you leave home, put your real-world, home-life behind you and put your "Mountain-Head" On and focus on whats ahead.

Practical matters - pre-departure

Family
1. I recommend you don't seek Approval only Forgiveness. Remember, for you, it may be a Dream, but for your family it may be a Nightmare that lasts 2 months, so try to be understanding, although you are indeed very selfish!. For myself, my family trekked with me part of the way and I safely returned them to Lukla and continued with the Expedition. Based on observations, I dont recommend you bring them all the way to Base Camp.
2. Make your WIll(s), especially the Asset Sheet Appendix. You may need in each Country you have Assets
3. Ensure sufficient Financial Reserves. Consider your Fixed Assets/Stocks, and if need to Liquidate them. You will realize there is no problem "jumping out of plane" and signing-up for Mt Everest - no excuses, please. Equally, if you don't return, then financial reserves to take care of family expenses and so forth.
4. Ensure your Partner aware your Investments and summarized.
5. Ensure your Partner can access your Investments in event of your expiration. Authorization to Sign, Passwords and so forth. In addition maybe consider making the bank accounts joint?

Work
1. Get Approval as far in advance as possible, suggest 6-12 months. If not approved, then consider Resigning. Remember there is "No Corporate Memory", dont let your grey Corporate Employer stop your Dreams. You have made an important decision, right? How badly do you want it? Don't let your Employer stop-it, you will probably be able to get another job, but maybe always live with the regret of not starting or reaching the Summit of Mt Everest, the Top of the World!
2. Suggest that you need a flexible working arrangement, to enable your Training.
3. Tell your Colleagues and Clients far in advance
4. Make a Plan for your absence
5. You will be able to return without the "wheels having fallen off"
6. If you are the Sole Director and 100% Shareholder of a Limited Company, consider whom will take-over or close-down the Business, in the event of your demise. It is

      much easier if you sign a letter in advance making another person a Director with Signing-rights (depending Country).
7. You will realize the World, Work, and People around you have not changed in 2 months, the World is still turning, but you have had a most memorable 2 months.

<u>Medical</u>.
1. It is both required by your Expedition Company and the Nepal Government to undertake a Medical and get a "Doctors Note". Now, I would also encourage you to take this more seriously and not simply get a "Doctors Note" that you are physically healthy (I note they don't ask about your mental state or sanity!). I undertook an additional full CT Scan to specifically check my Heart Arteries were clear. Thankfully they were surprisingly A1 and that provided further confidence - at least I was not likely to die of blocked arteries. This provision of extra confidence is a key point throughout this Guide, it's about reducing unknowns, one less thing or risk to worry about.
2. Dental check and resolve any lingering dental issues (since they may worsen at altitude). From observations it seems that any dental problems seen to worsen or expose themselves more at altitude. This can have a major impact on your ability to operate and may even end your Expedition. It is equally difficult to get effective dental treatment at BC or lower down the Valley – the string around the tooth extraction technique!.

Personal Gear, practical questions and stuff

Your clothing.
The key principle is layering. If you are too hot then take off the layers and vice-versa. Therefore you need to have the appropriate clothing and personal gear with you in your back back / daypack.

Secondly most of the time you will be wearing and using the same key pieces of clothing and personal equipment, therefore make sure you are happy with these. For example the major items include:
- 8000m boots and socks
- Leggings Base Layer
- Wind stopper Trousers (side zips essential and preferably pockets)
- Harness and associated personal equipment
- Upper Body Base Layer
- Fleece
- Mid-Layer Puffer Jacket
- Wind stopper Jacket
- Beanie
- Baseball Cap
- Buff
- Glasses
- Helmet
- Inner Gloves
- Mitts / Gloves
- Water Bottles (2 no.)
- Pee Bottle (1 no.)
- Personal Hygiene, Medicines, Foods, Torch Camera etc.
- Other smaller items
- Back-pack (which will also have your Sleeping Matt, Sleeping Bag etc.)

Only from C4 (or C3 depending weather) upwards will you really need to wear your Summit Suit and from C3 upwards be on Oxygen.

The following are **additional** points on your Personal Equipment List.

Baseball style Cap (or similar)
This simple item of clothing you will use most days on the expedition and is most critical, since will help prevent sun-burn and glare.
1. Ideally wide rim so protects most of your face
2. Neck and ear protection, mandatory
3. Neck strap so doesn't get blown-off, mandatory. You can sew your own strap if not provided.

Backpack(s)
I recommend two backpacks. A day-pack for trekking and Summit Night and a larger pack (which you can place packed into one of your duffles)
For the Summit rotation and especially Summit Night, a minimum 45L is required although upto 60L may be required, depending the size of the Oxygen Bottles your team is provided

with (check with your Company). A 45L will be able to contain all your items for day-trekking, including up the Khumbu Valley, and possibly Rest & Recovery Week.
Alternatively you could go with a single larger Backpack, minimum 60L upto 75L, although this is overkill for the trekking phases.
The key issue for the pack is that it should be lightweight and simple.

Booties
These are used within your tent, and optional. There are versions that have a robust sole and can be used to move around BC i.e. from your tent to Dining Tent. However, I suggest the real benefit is on Summit Night to put a spare, full 1-Litre bottle inside this and in your down-jacket or possibly day-pack. This will help reduce the time it takes for the bottle to freeze, which it will since temperature will be below -25c. I forgot, and my bottle was a 1-kilo weight which I could only use until the last two hours before arriving back at C4 (I had a 500ml fizzy drink inside my down jacket, which was adequate)

Boots (high-altitude)
You will buy an 8,000m double-boot however I would emphasise the critical importance of a good fit that is not tight, in fact slightly looser (you can wear extra pair of socks if really needed). You need to practice wearing with the sock(s) you will use on the mountain. I have observed other climbers with boots that were fractionally too tight really suffer higher up the Mountain, including frost-bite, resulting in the end of their expedition.

You should ideally keep your inner boots at the bottom of your sleeping bag.

Boredom
I recommend E-Books and better Audio Books. I recommend Audio Books since when you are in your sleeping bag it is difficult and cold to hold a mobile/tablet, whilst an audiobook is perfect, will put you to sleep and you can set a "sleep timer" (save battery also). For myself, as the weeks went by, I felt less bored and increasingly brain-dead as the normal activities of daily life at home and work drifted away into the distance. Perhaps this is what Retirement starts to feel like!...Perhaps after 2 months, you start becoming part of the natural environment around you.

Mini-Projector and Rollaway Screen.
This should be group equipment and do ask. These are mini in size now, high quality and typically USD300+ range. To watch Movies/Videos. Make sure you download and your Laptop or Phone and can connect to the Projector before departure. A white bed-sheet will equally suffice as projector screen in your Dining Tent.

Bottles (Drink and Pee)
You will bring a minimum 2 no. 1L bottles for drinks and 1 no. 1L for Pee (for men).

I recommend the thermal bottle covers, to keep drink warm or cold. This has added benefit that you can put between your legs in your sleeping bag without scolding yourself. The best place to warm your body more rapidly is to place the hot bottle next to your arteries by your groin i.e. in between your legs.

You need to practice using the Pee Bottle in your sleeping bag, a slip inside your bag will be traumatic – a true "Hamlet moment".

Do not leave any bottle with liquid outside your sleeping bag during the night, since will freeze solid and that will be another "Hamlet moment" when you need to pee!

Finally, if it cant get any worse, make sure you clearly identify your Drink and Pee bottles, because they are likely to be the same 1L bottles. The final "Hamlet moment". Myself after returning at night from a long day, exhausted from on an expedition in Tibet in the dark I took several very big gulps down, only to realise....my pee was pure and it honestly didnt taste or smell of pee, but...

Buff
Bring two Buff. This simple item of clothing you will use most days on the expedition and is most critical, since will help prevent dust and reduce cold, dry air entering your mouth. If you lose one, it will be a serious problem.

Cash.
Bring more then you expect, you can bring it back.
1. The largest additional Cash requirement will be for Helicopters, followed by Tip Money. I estimate the allowance of USD2,000 for Helicopters.
2. In Namche, there are several ATM Machines that allow you to withdraw USD100 for a USD5 Fee. These ATM Machines are not reliable and in great demand.
3. There is a very good method for receiving up to USD1,000 per day, for a USD5 charge at a very good Exchange Rate - "Western Union". There are at least two Bank locations in Namche, both signposted, where you can arrange this and the Transfer is done in minutes. I used this method myself very successfully and recommend it. You do not need any complicated prior Account Set-Up Arrangement and simply bring your Passport to the Bank (not a copy of Passport page) to register your details when doing the transaction. Simply, you register, the person in the remote country goes to a WU outlet and provides the Cash to Transfer and your name/country location. Minutes later it shows on the Namche Bank WU computer and you can withdraw the money in Namche (same applies to other locations in Nepal). Rock n Roll, party-on, but try not to blow it all in Namche...

Crampons
Steel Crampons and make sure they are sharpened.
Make sure you try and can fit the Crampons with your large 8,000m Boots and they are not too small. Equally, practice putting them on (at night, in snow and so forth) and correctly using the straps – no loose ends to get caught on and go tumbling over. You need to be able to tighten them properly and monitor / check as you are moving. I also recommend a special crampon carrying bag, else the crampon will rip into your expensive clothing in your duffle.

Cellular Phone – Telephony and Data.
4. Generally, there is acceptable Voice coverage along the route, including Base Camp, with reducing Data / Internet Services.
5. Buy at least 2 no. SIM cards from different Telco Providers in Kathmandu. It's cheap.
6. Also bring your home-country SIM, as a further option. However, over 2 months, it will be considerably cheaper to buy local
7. Buy a package with both Data, Voice, and SMS. Check the cost of International Outbound Calling - it can be incredibly cheap and the Voice Service is more reliable

then Data, especially past Namche and specifically in Base Camp, so at least you can talk to people overseas (and locally).
8. In addition, I recommend buying a WIFI personal hot-spot gadget that connects to any available Cellular Network and is typically fixed-price for a large amount of Bandwidth. This will work along the valley ie. anywhere there is cellular coverage. This will work globally, so a good investment.
9. Satellite Phone. This is expensive to buy and not essential. Your Expedition Leader will have a Sat Phone. The reality is that you will likely need to use when you send an SMS or phone call from C4 to tell your loved ones that you have Summitted ! In an emergency also and this is your choice, whether you want this extra "insurance" or "nice to have". On our expedition, only the Team Leader had a Sat Phone and no issues. You should talk months in advance to your local Telecon Companies about Rental Options. For example, in Hong Kong, I could have rented a Sat Phone for USD 20 per week.

Duffles
I recommend 2 no. 100L duffles, maximum. This size will be more then adequate and if full then you are probably taking too much stuff! However your Expedition Company may have restrictions including weight and you should check. Note, you can place your larger backpack, full, inside one of the duffles.
You should have name tags and your name and Expedition Company marked very clearly on the bags i.e. written on masking tape and taped to side of duffles.

"Crocs" or equivalent .- for BC primarily.
1. Yes, I am serious. Robust, lightweight, easy to slip on/off particularly when getting in/out of the tent, which you will do often and this becomes a hassle putting on trainers or boots. My Crocs also had a "furry" inside which were warm, particularly with socks and no issue in the evenings in the Dining Tent

Day-Pack - 45 Litre
1. A 45 L day-pack will both be adequate for your Approach Trek to BC and all the way to the Summit (depending the size of your O bottles).
2. A Pack with side punches for 1 L drink bottles is strongly recommended
3. A Pack with a zip-opening top section on the outside is strongly recommended
4. When you switch to Oxygen, depending on the size of Oxygen Bottles provided, a 45 L day-pack can comfortably hold the bottle. If larger Bottles, you will be forced to use your heavier and larger main Back Pack, depends on your Expedition Oxygen provisioning.

Ear Plugs
1. Recommend the silicon gel type rather than cheaper airplane give-way types. Bring a couple of pairs.
2. This will be useful for the trek to BC and the noisy lodges, BC and beyond.

Go-Bag
Next to your sleeping bag, particularly beyond BC, you will need small items that you frequently need to access, without wanting to fumble around or lose small items in the mess of your tent, particularly when its dark. These items include Head-Torch, toothpaste, mini-tissues, wet-wipes, throat lozenges, personal medicine, phone and so forth. A large zip-lock back is sufficient also.

Handwarmers
These can be used for your hands or also within your Boots. There are different types. Do not assume these will be a panacea to cold, they may not work very well, especially at the higher altitudes. Keeping on your inner clothing and applying Oxygen from your tank will also help when you are ready to use.

Harness
A standard, modern, lightweight Rock Climbing Harness will be good. The key is to be able to put the strap through the buckle in the front with your clothes on, especially over a Down Jacket (and then importantly double-back the strap thrugh the buckle!). You should practice putting on your harness as if you are at C3, C4 i.e. inside your tent whilst wearing your down suit. The same applies to your other personal equipment i.e. using whilst wearing your Down Jacket.

Helicopters
These are like Private Taxis in the Khumbu.

This links to my YouTube channel (Michael Tomordy) with several Helicopter Videos, including Lukla to Namche and Namche to Everest Base Camp.

https://www.youtube.com/channel/UCbSdIo2vXU1GwhIdGwum8Tw

The Price is market-driven and similar between the several Operators. Everyone will become an agent for Helicopter Services, so don't be concerned! I strongly recommend you use Helicopters if you can afford it, they save both Time, reduce Risk and more importantly Save Personal Energy.

I strongly do not recommend using choppers whilst you are in the Approach phase or at a Stage that could be deemed necessary for Acclimatisation, Training or Fitness i.e. as a way to reduce going up-hill on your approach to Base Camp or flying from Camp 1 to Base Camp.

For example,
- In the final "rest-week" we walked to Pheriche (about 6+ hours) and chartered a Heli to Namche. We then used Heli from Namche to Base Camp. This both saved considerable Time and Energy. The cost was approximately USD 1,000 return.
- Chartered a Helicopter from Base Camp to Kathmandu directly after we reached the Base Camp following Summit. The cost was approximately USD 3000 for 5 persons. The Heli stopped in Namche for a night or two and then to Kathmandu in about 1 hour. This compares to a 3-5 day hike out, not mentioning the possibility of bad weather in Lukla and delays to Flights.
- You should budget minimum USD2,000 for Helicopters

Hiking Boots or Trainers?
You can trek to BC in robust trainers, but I would not recommend it unless you also have ankle-height hiking boots packed. The risk of using trainers is primarily if it snows on the trail (although a low probability) and secondly risk of twisting ankle, which is more likely.

Head Torch
A standard head Torch will suffice, with spare batteries. Lithium batteries are better and recommended for your Summit-push rotation, although more costly. However you may wish

to also bring a second, more sophisticated head-torch for the Summit Rotation, this is Optional. Specifically, the type that has a separate battery pack that you can place inside your down jacket. These have the benefit of a larger battery pack, importantly longer lasting since also kept warm and more powerful beam options. This is for "worst case" scenario of bad-weather and a longer stay than expected on the Summit Push. These are more costly, in the USD125 range.

In addition, you may find useful to have a small light for use inside the tent that is hanging from inside the tent. It will provide general light coverage and practically more beneficial, simpler, faster then using your torch (and save your valuable torch batteries).

Hoodie for BC.
Optional. You should practice sleeping with a buff over your face at home/camping, which you may find difficult. I find that a loose-fitting Hoodie is less suffocating and keep your head warm. Alternatively, I also used a Merino Wool base layer with an in-built hoodie. The most critical aspect in your tent is the cold, dry air at night. This may result in you getting a cold, runny nose, blocked-up, sore throat etc. These are serious problems on the mountain - try to minimize the risk, they are hard to get rid off.

Himalayan Rescue Association (HRA) - BC Medical clinic
There is a medically qualified staff in this clinic tent near the start of the Ice Fall.
For USD 100 per season, you can visit as many times as you wish for a Consultation. Any medicines, anything, is an extra charge. This is well worth the upfront fee since the fee also goes to supporting your Sherpas and Porters at BC. If you dont pay upfront and need advice then you can pay on-the-spot, although may work out more expensive.

Ice Axe and Trekking Pole
You will be required to bring these, however beyond BC you may not actually need to choose them or very infrequently. This includes on your Summit rotation. For myself the benefit is potentially on descending and as a climbing-aid on the descent, but again, I very rarely used either. If you feel you will use for descending then a longer Ice Axe is preferable, given the relatively steep angles above C2.

Insurance
There are a variety of Insurances that you will require, including:
1. Helicopter Rescue (mandatory), although not strictly Insurance. We had a situation where a Member was rescued twice by Helicopter (BC and C2) at different times in the same Expedition and taken to Kathmandu. The Rescue Company advised they could rescue as many times as needed in a season provided not the same reason for evacuation! Check your Insurance Policy.
2. Travel Insurance (optional). This could cover lost luggage or change in flight type issues, which are real possibilities.
3. Trip Cancellation Insurance (optional). Yes, this may happen either before the Expedition or during. It is certainly possible that your Expedition Company cancels the Expedition, whilst on the Mountain due to mountain conditions or related, and possibly yourself. This happened whilst we were at Everest in 2014, as a result of the Avalanche and loss of life.

Internet. You need multiple solutions.

1. You will spend a lot of time getting frustrated on the Mountain due to lack of Data and Internet access. You will want to update your social media, email and chat to friends about your heroics.
2. Internet. You will be able to buy WIFI scratch-cards along the Khumbu Trail, including Base Camp that you can use with most WIFI type personal devices. Remember if you buy a card in Pheriche it is unlikely to work at Base Camp and vice-versa. The service quality decreases and the price seems to increase as you get closer to Base Camp. The service is unreliable, relatively costly and you will get frustrated, but you have limited options. There was a reliable rumor that at Base Camp the Data Service on the Telephone Networks was disabled so that people were required to buy the more expensive WIFI Scratch Cards since the Data Service at Base Camp frequently did not work. This is Nepal.

Laptop/Netbook – mini ruggedised
You may wish to consider bringing a mini Netbook
This should be SSD storage and be ruggedised. There will be times when you may wish to type or view content on a larger screen, for example in your R&R week. A long battery life would be a key requirement also.

Masking Tape / "Plumber Black Tape"
This will be a life-saver when you don't expect it. Essential. You can use this most importantly when your personal equipment or clothing has a failure or you need to strap your pole to a climber's broken leg and tape it up, rigid. Now, you need the tape when you have a failure. The items you will have with you all the time are, your drink bottles, pee-bottle, and maybe your Ice Axe (I say maybe Ice Axe, since in reality you are unlikely to use the Axe and may be advised not to bring beyond BC, subject to your Expedition Company advice). I tape a reasonable amount of tape around my Bottles and Ice Axe for such emergencies (it also doesn't add any weight).

Mountain Boot Spare Laces
As per the Plumber's Tape above, this will be a life-saver when you don't expect it. Essential. Don't ignore this small item and think you will never use it. "Para Cord" is similar, stronger but not suitable for your boots. You can use this not only if your laces snap but when your personal equipment or clothing has a failure. This is small and lightweight and you can keep both at BC and in your BackPack when ascending/descending.

I learned this lesson the hard way when both my boot heels semi-detached along with the crampons, in in the Ice Fall at 0200 in 2017. We temporary repaired the boots in the Ice Fall with mountain boot shoe laces and I continued to C1 where Plumber Tape was used to wrap the crampons to the boots semi-permanently. This also proved that its possible, although not normal practice, to keep your crampons on, rather then take-off the boots each evening.

Name Tags (and "dog tags")
All your Duffles should have a clear Name Tag attached. Equally, your Name and Expedition Company also marked in large letters (can be written on masking tape and attached to the side of Duffles)

Oxygen
1. Oxygen is your great friend. It will improve your chances of success, especially if this may be your only attempt then buying more is better then less or the minimum. It will make you feel warmer, think clearer, move more quickly and so

forth. If you have not used O's before then nothing to worry about. It is not like Scuba and far more comfortable experience, no comparison.
2. The O's will be on "constant flow" and the good news is you can breathe any way you wish without any constraint i.e. how you normally breathe on the mountain. The O mask will fit comfortably over your face and you will manage to sleep with it on and O's flowing. At rest in your tent or "asleep", you will reduce the flow-rate, maybe down to 1 lpm or less. As you are going uphill, perhaps 2 lpm. Depending your available O's and exhaustion level this may be increased to 3 lpm or even 4 lpm, but not for the entire duration. It really depends on how you feel, how much O's left and what your Leader/Sherpa suggest.
3. Whilst the Sherpa will help you to manage your O supply it is worthwhile learning the basics at Base Camp. This should include:
    a. Changing a Bottle, just in case you need to by yourself.
    b. the Flow Rate,
    c. How much O is left in the tank and is the O actually flowing correctly and Regulator Working.
    d. the Oxygen Tube may detach from your mask, so learn how to put back into the mask, which is easy enough, but need to take your outer gloves/mitts off. These are all simple enough tasks.
4. You will likely use O's 24/7 after Camp 3 to the Summit, and the return to Camp 3 or lower if you have spare. Do not be a Hero and try operating without it, except when eating/drinking/talking for short while etc. Do not go to "the toilet" at Camp 4 without your O's - it will be hard enough already!
5. Depending on the Expedition Company and size of bottles, 5 no. Bottles are typical. I purchased 7 no. Smaller or standard size bottles, which was more than adequate, including an extra, unforeseen day at Camp 4 on the ascent. The cost per bottle was approximately USD500. I recommend you buy extra pre-departure, in case of delay at the higher camps.

Personal Food - general
Work on the assumption that the food in Base Camp and onwards will not be good, in fact rather bland and even "bad", especially after a few weeks. Try all the personal food/drink you will eat before your expedition whilst Training
1. You will likely eat mostly Carbo (in the form of Rice, Pasta, Potatoes). One night you may be served Spagetti with Tomato Sauce and the next night Tomato Sauce with Spagetti.
2. There will be inadequate Protein and Fat
3. The food will likely be monotonous and not tasty
4. On the expedition, you will also lose Muscle since you are unlikely to get enough Protein, therefore think about maximizing Protein intake at any opportunity. This is possible in Namche in your rest week also. I can strongly recommend the "Yak Sizzler".

Example of Drinks
1. Sports Drinks, both the powder and especially the tablet form (since smaller and more practical, less messy then if powder spills out). There are many types and brands and I suggest its more about your personal preference based upon what you normally use.
2. Coffee. If you are a coffee drinker, I recommend you bring your favorite grind, maximum strength Expresso powder to save powder, contained within a metailsed Container to keep fresh over 2 months (there is one Italian brand that offers this).

In addition as a minimum a French Press (ruggedized). Beyond this, I recommend a small-size Italian Coffee Maker that you would boil on a stove at home. The camping gas you can buy in Namche. You will enjoy your morning coffee outside the dining tent (and make your fellow Climbers very jealous!). Also, for Summit Push I blended coffee with my fizzy drink at BC. Also, note that caffeine may help with fat metabolism.
3. Fizzy sugar drink specifically for Summit Push and as a treat in BC (Namche, Gorek Shep and at BC you can purchase)

Examples of Food to bring, that may not be in your List (try all food before purchasing). These are designed to be tasty and provide calories and salts. The below items are durable, lightweight and small in size.
1. Personally, I cannot stand the freeze-dried food that you add boiled water too and is sold in the outdoor shops. MRE - the meal is pre-cooked and boil-in-the-bag concept, hence your Sherpa / Cook need to place in boiling water in the Cook Tent for 2 minutes. These Meals are much harder to purchase but much tastier, solid and good calories
2. Packet Soups (Powder). The cup size portion recommended. These are tasty, 1-200 calories, lightweight, easy to make and a cahnge from the often provided packets of "Ramen noodles".
3. "Meal Replacement Drink" packets. These are 2-300 calories, drink hot or cold. This enables you to get a lot of calories quickly thru a drink. Bring from home.
4. Cheese (processed, packaged type) Provide Fat primarily. You can buy in Kathmandu and Namche but less choice. Bring initial "best supply" from home and resupply in Kathmandu or Namche. Processed, tasty, lightweight, does not "go bad".
5. Sausage (processed, packaged type) - fat and protein primarily. Processed, tasty, lightweight, does not "go bad". Bring from home, since generally not available in Nepal
6. Beef Jerky or "Biltong". Dried beef jerky in packets. High in protein and calories, lightweight and tasty snack. You can buy in KTM.
7. Peanuts (in packets). Perhaps a 1kg mixed-nut bottle for base camp. You will appreciate the salt and taste.
8. You need Energy / Chocolate Bars that provide the most Calories/Energy for the smallest weight/size. Consider FlapJack type bars also, approximately 400 calories per bar, although these are drier to eat and need to be washed down. Remember they will freeze so keep close to your body closer to eating time
9. Condiments. The soups and meals served may not be to your taste and become monotonous. Examples to add flavor, "Seaweed sheets", Chilli Pepper and so forth.
10. Figs or equivalent dried fruits. These are already dried so no issue going bad. These provide Carbo, calories and fill your stomach. These do not become rock-hard like a chocolate bar.
11. Crisps (in the round tube). Taste great, Carbo, calories and salt. Lightweight and robust container. A further tip is to consider "crushing crisps" in Namche and placing in mini zip-lock bags. You will be amazed how much more space efficient this method is and a higher amount of calories etc
12. "Fizzy Drink". You can buy at Namche or BC. This is a treat, a welcome change from glacier water and electrolyte, a real boost, but strongly recommended for the Summit Push.

13. **Personally Hydrated Food.** If you really want to eat tasty, "space-age" food, and impress your team-mates then consider this advanced option. You need a special dehydration machine at home and can dehydrate and shrink-wrap into bags all manner of fruits and vegetables. Once rehydrated, they taste almost as fresh as when picked from the farm (seriously). You can add re-hydrated Strawberries to your morning porridge or Brocolli to your evening meals.

Personal Solar Panel
1. Bring your own
    a. Attach to backpack
    b. Multi cable adaptor that you can charge phone or battery
    c. Some have batteries that also double-up as a torch (recommended)
2. Bring a mini-solar also, suitable for mobile phone (optional)

Photo family / loved ones
Sealed in plastic that can keep in a pocket. Momentos photos etc that you can Stick or hang in your tent, like Christmas tree bobbles!. You can take this all the way to the Summit. Alternatively you make take the view to not bring anything that reminds you of home, so that you can get your "Mountain-head on" and focus.

Photocopies
Bring extra copies of your passport pages, permits and Insurance, including Helicopter Rescue details (and Membership number). In addition bring passport photos (minimum 4 no.).

Pillow for BC
You need to sleep and it will be less than ideal. A large, soft, comfortable pillow that you use in your bed at home will help (yes, I know it sounds soft, it is, literally!). Also, bring smaller travel pillow for the trek to BC whilst in Lodges.

Plastic "sandwich" box
In your BC tent you will have lots of small items that you need to keep together in a central place close to your head for easy access from your sleeping bag (and your tent will likely become a mess). For example, medicines, toilet paper/wet wipes, torch, camera, phone, leads, chargers and so forth. A large, flat sandwich type box is ideal. Be careful to pack carefully in your duffle.

Shaving.
Do I need to Shave for Summit Week? Subjective. The argument is that ice will form on your beard. Myself, I did not shave. If you wish to shave then Namche is the best option, else it is likely to be a troublesome and painful exercise if you try it yourself (or ask a friendly Yak herder to use his shears!).

Sleeping bag.
Bring two. One for BC (5000m+ rated) and one for beyond BC, up to 8000m+ / Summit rated. Don't get a "straight jacket". You need space to move around

Sleeping Mat and mattress
You need two Mats for the expedition. I recommend the "Thermarest" or equivalent with the hexagonal arrangement to trap air. For Base Camp, you will also need either your own blow-up mattress, which has a risk of puncture, from home or better you can purchase a minimum

of 2 no. 3" foam mattress, either thru your Expedition Company or Namche Bazar (less supply in Namche).

Tarpaulin (lightweight) for C1 (this should be Group Equipment)
Inside your C1 tent, the temperature may rise to plus 40c, as it did on our Expedition, and you will both cook and go "berserk". I strongly recommend your team brings a tarpaulin that connects between the tents to shelter you from the sun and enable group members to sit outside whilst avoiding the sun.

Ski Goggles and Glacier Glasses
Glacier Glasses. You will use these everyday and essential item of personal equipment. Make sure they have the neck strap. Recommend bringing a second emergency pair of glasses.
Ski Goggles. Most of the time you will not need them, except most likely for bad-weather conditions, therefore you must bring them and contain in a hardened case to avoid crushing in your duffle (which has happened to myself).

For both glasses and goggles it is critical that you should check UV rating suitable for the high-altitude, your normal ski goggles may not be and typically for low-altitude and skiing. We had two persons with Snow Blindness at 8,000m and possible eye-wear "failure" contributed to this.

Tip: bring the anti-fog cream/gel that Skiers use. It is very likely your glasses/goggles will fog, including when using the Buff or if use at night (yes you may use at night, if bad weather or slight wind, especially Summit night).

Personal Medicine
Again, follow the list given by the Expedition, these are additional comments. You will bring more then you need and hopefully not use most of it, which you can bring home. Do not rely on Team Medical Supplies, you must bring your own personal supply. However, ensure that for the most common ailments you bring more than needed, since it is often these common ailments that will worsen and impact your performance. Specifically, I strongly recommend

1. 2 x bottles Dry Cough Medicine (you can use this as a preventative and take a spoon-a-day, if spare)
2. A large number of Throat Lozenges with extra medicine included (these are extra strength and medicated not normal strength)
3. Asthma type Inhaler. This can be beneficial in dealing with the cold, dry air (optional)
4. Ibufrofen tablets. Aches, pains and strains
5. Diarrhea tablets or powder, including considering using at C3 or above.
6. Decongestant. This is to clear your throat/nose of mucus and flem. Specifically, bring the menthol type liquid drops that you can use in boiling water and cover your head with a towel at BC. Also, Nose Menthol Inhaler or similarly help clear.
7. Triple-Action Headache/Cold, Fever, Mucus tablets
8. Antibiotic for respiratory and stomach. Stronger stuff when normal medicines not working.
9. MultiVitamins, 60 tablets. Take daily.
10. Wet Wipes. In addition to toilet paper (no need to bring from home per say), this will be a cleaner "finish" when you have done your business. Also for hand, face, other cleaning
11. Hemorrhoid Cream...you can also buy in Namche

12. Hand-Towel (and soap) for personal washing. You can keep clean and fresh by washing in a bowl or BC Shower Tent.
13. Deodorant Spray / Roll-On.

A word on Diamox. I have both used and not used Diamox on Expeditions. A common school of thought is to take Diamox daily from arrival in Kathmandu. On my Mt Everest Expedition, I did not once take Diamox or any other altitude drugs and I had no negative effects and my performance was not impaired.

A word on Dexamethasone (HACE) and Nifedipine (HAPE). These should be considered for descending rather then using to aid your ascent. You should consult your Expedition Company on whether you need to bring a very small personal supply or whether the Company will provide.

Thermos (mini)
Most of the time you will not use a Thermos. However it can be particularly useful on the Summit-night, when unless bottle is inside your 8000m Suit it will freeze or at the high camps.

Tip Money.
Some Expeditions collect Tip Money in advance at Kathmandu, regardless of what happens, do check (!). You can assume USD800 for your personal Sherpa and maybe USD 500 for others, minimum.

Watch
A normal, analog watch is acceptable (and what I normally wear). You do not need a fancy, top-of-range GPS Watch since many people around you will have these watches and you will easily be able to know the Altitude, the primary feature. The day before my departure my wife kindly bought me the most expensive GPS watch on the market. Interestingly I found the pulse-rate feature the most beneficial and constantly monitored this and regulated my pace accordingly, to keep pulse "low". Also, the GPS Track completely failed around Camp 4 and shows me going in a straight line from the South Col into Tibet, almost levitating myself and flying - impossible! Perhaps it was not designed for this altitude and getting confused with GPS signals on the border at this high altitude.

9. Physical Training – Train Harder to climb Easier

There is an Army expression "Train Hard to Fight Easy". The same principle applies to your Mt Everest expedition. Everest will involve tough physical exertion at an extreme altitude which will require good preparation. **Physical Endurance and Resilience are most critical and the ability to move at a steady, "slow" pace for long duration over multiple consecutive days**. Being knackered is arguably one of the most controllable constraints that will stop you summiting and something you can train to avoid happening. If you are physically exhausted this will send a signal to your Brain that you cannot go on, you will be forced to rest at best or potentially go no further and Quit. Therefore as a Baseline make sure your Endurance and Resilience levels are suitably high. You don't want to fail on the Mountain because you were not fit enough - that's just down to lack of the right training at home. A bad excuse.

Ideally your goal should be to Train Harder then what you are likely to face most of the time on Mt Everest, then Rest and Recover, although no training will truly prepare you for 8000m and beyond and the unique challenges that you will face to do with Altitude, Weather and so forth. Most of your training will be well below your perceived limits. You may need to go to your perceived Maximum Limit and then beyond your Maximum Limit into what I call the Danger Zone, in a controlled, safe manner - this is as much mental as physical limits. You need to be ready to face challenges, to know what you are capable of and not be shocked for the first time – test yourself in advance elsewhere.

This principle also applies to Acclimatisation, which you will only start once you arrive at Lukla - go higher then descend and rest on your rotations. **How well you acclimatise is one of the most critical factors in determining your success and equally whether you will become ill - focus on this critical success factor, the process starts from when you arrive in Lukla**.
There are Fit people whom are Acclimatised and Summit, equally there are Less Fit people whom are Acclimatised and Summit, however there are No climbers whom Summit whom are Not Acclimatised – it doesnt matter How fit you are or what high degree of experience or expertise you have, if you are not acclimatised you are very unlikely to Summit. This is therefore so critical as a success factor.

The real test will come when the going gets tough and you can't manage your emotions.

What type of training?

If you were going to do a Marathon then you will do a lot of running, if you are doing long distance cycle race you will do a lot of cycling, if you are going to swim the English Channel, you will be swim-training in the English Channel. You understand therefore that to o climb Mt Everest you need to do Hill Training and mixed with some Alpine and Altitude - it's common-sense. Furthermore, you should make your training as close to what you may experience on Mt Everest, in terms of stress on your body i.e. duration, load, and intensity (including altitude, albeit not 8848m!).

My observation is that many beginners do the physical and technical training, because it is easier to achieve, **however climbers often do not spend enough time gaining high-**

altitude experience, which is so important. The reason may be that to gain 6 - 7000m+ experience will take 3 - 4 weeks minimum, a relatively long duration. Do not take short-cuts and think that you dont need to go to these altitudes previously - there are clear mental and physical benefits.

Your Training should be Specific to the goal and at a similar pace and intensity i.e. hill training for Mt Everest. I should at this point add that Specific Training equally applies to the Technical alpine skills you would need. In fact, you can combine Mountain Specific Physical and Technical Training together on short-duration mountain training trips. You need to adapt your aerobic training for Mt Everest i.e. endurance for high-altitude, rather than a fast-paced, short distance bike ride. Myself, I only did Hill Training with weight and general Hiking - I did not do any running, cycling, swimming, strength training, gym or pilates. Indirectly, Core training, which is obtained from hill training with a weighted backpack. If you feel that your upper body needs strengthening then consider Gym-work, specifically to simulate pulling on the line, which may be beneficial whilst using the Jumar, although I did not do any gym / upper-body muscle strengthening. It is possible you do not have any hills nearby and those other fitness activities will certainly suffice. Equally, a variety of training may remove monotony of Training and enhanced training benefit, but I still believe core training should be in the hills with weight, if possible.

You need a Baseload Fitness Programme and once you have achieved a good base level of fitness, introduce more Mountaineering Specific Training. Design your training specifically for Mt Everest and ensure it is of a higher intensity then base-load fitness training. Doing aerobic training like running, swimming, cycling will create the baseload but specific training will, for example, be endurance focused and primarily hill training. This base training requires Volume training i.e. total hours/days per week and will increase your capacity aerobic work and also prepare your body for mountaineering strength and endurance training.

The mountain will require you to use both aerobic and anaerobic channels for walking. Simply put aerobic converts oxygen to energy, whilst anaerobic energy can be produced with less oxygen – as we know the higher you go the less oxygen is available.

Simply put I recommend
1. Hill Training/Hiking with Weight (gradually increasing to maximum 15kg backpack and 1.5kg Ankle Weights),
2. Medium/Long Duration (gradually increasing), 5 - 10 hours minimum, mixed with longer, upto 16 hour hill hikes closer to departure date.
3. Multi-Day and
4. Low/Medium Intensity (and shallow breathing, rapid recovery). You should be able to keep going for a long time.

Most of your training should be focussed on long duration, low-to moderate-intensity to provide the aerobic fitness required. If you are doing long duration, hill training, with weight at low intensity then this may take up to 48 hours to recover and strengthen your body and enable the restoration of glycogen stores. Therefore you are looking at 3 no. Long duration training days per week maximum. In the last 2 - 3 months you should also be doing more multi-day, long-duration, low-intensity hill training.

Your Training Programme should be structured and planned.
Your Mountaineering Specific Training should gradually increase in duration, load and intensity (but don't make too intense at the expense of achieving longer duration and time).

However, it should be mixed with easier, maintenance Hikes/Training (for rest, recovery and strengthening) and equally Longer, harder more epic Hikes. Simply put, you gradually need to increase your training load but also have easier days mixed into the schedule.

For example about a 3 weeks before leaving, I complete the Wilson Trail in Hong Kong by myself. This is 80km, very rugged hilly, mostly remote terrain with lots of up/down elevation and took 20 hours non-stop. This was a Psychology boost as much as an endurance/resilience training. You should gradually increase the training load and allow time for your body to adapt. This should be part of a structured training plan

Structured Training Plan with Goal setting.
A structured training plan with Goal setting as an integral part during your months of training will make your training and achieving outcomes more efficient. Ideally, a written plan however at least a mental summary to check your progression.

Endurance Training is critical. Having Resilience is critical.
Your efforts will need to be maintained for a minimum of a few hours upto 15+ hours, however, it will need to last for several days and in the case of the Summit Week, literally 7+ days of progressively more difficult and exhausting daily activity.

If you imagine the Summit-night, the total duration from C4 to Summit and return to C4 may be 14 - 20 hours, with little rest. The Day before you will ascend from C3 to C4 for say 7+ hours and a few hours rest and then go for the Summit. Therefore you should practice hiking for 24 hours non-stop.

Hill Climbing/Hiking - essential
You don't have a hill or mountain nearby then improvise. It is more likely that you have a tall building with a staircase. You can do multiple repetitions.

Weighted Backpack and Ankle Weights (with Hill Climbing) - strongly recommended
You will be wearing and carrying weight above BC and load-carrying during training is a well understood military training concept. It will place a strain on your body but also strengthen your calf, leg muscles, and core whilst improving your aerobic performance. It will also enhance your muscular endurance. It will force you to hike slowly and more deliberately, with a similar pulse rate, like how you will walk on the mountain. You will be able to practice other techniques that you will use on the Mountain, notably for example the Rest Step and Pressure Breathing. However it is also exhausting to always carry weight on each hill climbing session, so sometimes hill hike without weight.

In summary:
1. Weighted Backpack. I recommend no more than 15kg, in fact, the maximum extra weight you will carry maybe 10kg+, including your clothing, harness etc. so you are already training harder
    a. Carrying several 6 Litre (6kg) water bottles is best since you can easily empty the water at the top of the hill to save your knees on the descent. If the potable water you can also drink it, particularly useful in an emergency situation.
    b. You should mix-up your training since it is hard work to train constantly with weight, rest and strengthen your body.
    c. Too much weight will have a detrimental effect on your training and is potentially risky. If you have too much weight it will be harder to achieve

a Training Effect, because you may not be able to complete your training session and not put in the long distance, duration, intensity that is required. Secondly, if you fall over with 20kg on your back it may result in injury.
2. Ankle Weights: Your Mountaineering Boots will weigh about 1.5kg. Your Crampons will weigh 1kg. I regularly wore 1.5kg ankle weights whilst training, in addition to weight backpack. There is always a training opportunity and so I also wore my ankle weights during the day, on the Metro system, on the Bus, at Business Meetings and in the Pub (not every day!).

Hill Sprinting / Interval Training.
This is difficult and you should do maybe once per week. This will over-stress your heart, lungs, and legs, but make you stronger (and require rest/recovery time). It is also very satisfying and motivational. There is the classic Interval Hill Running but other methods also. Myself, I preferred to jog on an uphill paved trail without stopping, variable angle, about 15-20 degree, in about 20 minutes. This would take me 60 minutes at walking pace.

Listen to your body.
How do you feel today? Adapt and adjust your training accordingly. This requires you to monitor and have the flexibility to change the plan.

Rest and Recovery.
This is as important as the Training. It is during this period during your training that your body becomes stronger. When you train hard you put your body under stress and it weakens, however during the rest and recovery period your body strengthens further.

Tapering-off.
In the few weeks prior to departure you should taper-off your training to maintenance fitness/hiking at most, and importantly avoid injury, stay healthy, rest and allow you to put on weight and spend the time getting your life in order. Your body will recover and strengthen from the excess training stress it has been placed under. You need to consolidate those hard months of training and critically not get an injury or illness prior to departure.

Your Body Weight and Supplements
I lost about 10% of my body-weight, about 8kg, it is a certainty that you will lose weight. Therefore I recommend you put on body weight pre-departure. This can simply be eating more of the same at home, especially when you taper-off your training near the end. I was 75kg on departure and about 67kg at the end. You don't want to become overweight and equally, you should already be at a high level of fitness at the departure date from home. You will lose both muscle and fat. You are likely to put on more weight as fat at home, which is ok and better then muscle-mass.

There is a school of thought that talks about the benefit of for more red blood cells in order to improve Oxygen transportation, which acclimatisation aims to achieve. It was suggested to me to take an Iron supplement for 60 days prior to help with red blood cell production. I am not sure if this worked since I did a blood test prior to departure and my red blood cell count levels were not especially high.

Eating for Training

Eat well; you are not on a weight-loss programme. A balanced, healthy diet is the simple advice during you 6 – 12-month preparation phase. You need to ensure you don't lose too much weight, arguably being slightly heavier than normal pre-departure, as I have explained.

Ideally, you need to learn and train to burn Fat rather than only sugars or Carbo; since your body has considerably more fat (100,000+ calories) stores then sugar stores (2000+ calories). There are certain diet regimes that may help this. You need to be able to perform on less Carbo (especially then you may train with at home), over a multi-day, endurance cycle. Long duration and Low-Intensity training and mountaineering on Mt Everest is typically in the 65%+ range of your maximum heart rate, which should enable your body to learn to use Fat since Carbo energy is consumed for more faster, higher intensity workouts, which is not the type of training being recommended.

Your body has very little sugar stores, which are for short duration activity. However, Fat is stored in much larger quantities, and even more for those whose training is focused on achieving endurance i.e. yourself. Fat also contains double the energy compared to sugar. My regular "maintenance hiking" morning routine about 3 times a week, would consist waking up and hiking uphill with the weighted pack for 1+ hour on an empty stomach, having a coffee and returning home for simple breakfast. Thereby I am also getting my body used to burning Fat first. For more serious longer-duration 8+ hour hikes I would have a bigger breakfast 1+ hour prior to start e.g. baked beans on toast, egg, a cup of tea, juice (almost the full-English breakfast without the sausage!). I then eat little and often e.g. muesli/energy bars (2 no.), bananas (2 no.), and maybe pasta (if I know high-intensity, hill-climbing) and drinking 4+ liters of sports drink over the duration – small amounts of Carbo over a long duration. I also bring emergency Salts for mixing with a drink if I get badly dehydrated and 2 no. Energy Gel.

ALTITUDE
EXPERIENCE

Your Training

PHYSICAL
FITNESS

TECHNICAL
SKILLS

10. Technical Training - Alpine

I recommend that it would be preferable to gradually build-up over time the skills and experience required, rather in say the last 6 - 12 months. This skills build-up over several years will be less stressful and will often be great adventures on different peaks in far-flung places on this wonderful planet, that you would not oridinarily visit as a tourist. It is this long journey over years that creates your personal body of knowledge and skill. You may be able to summit with minimal technical skills or experience but surely a build-up over years would ultimately lower the risk, be more satisfying, make your expedition more enjoyable, make you appreciate better and respect Mt Everest more.

I recommend that you increase and refresh your Alpine Technical Training / Skills at least 6 months prior to your departure. This doesn't mean start from zero Alpine experience and I would recommend that you have prior alpine technical experience, whether Himalaya or lower elevation mountain ranges. You may have read that "Mt Everest is not the most technical mountain". However it is the ability to have the necessary technical skills to get you out of a difficult situation in the event that something does go wrong or you are faced with a situation, even if a low probability.

The objective of gaining Alpine Climbing Experience is primarily not Altitude rather practice and gaining confidence in your technical skills, movement and with your Mountaineering Personal equipment in a lower altitude, "lower-risk", more comfortable Alpine environment. The other benefit of lower altitude training is that typically day-trips and staying in relatively comfortable accommodation with home comforts, rather than a tent.

Ideally, your specific alpine training should match the technical skills needed for Mt Everest so that you can get your body and mind used to the skills, equipment, difficulties, and risks. If you are not near an Alpine environment that enables long weekends, then Christmas is normally a long holiday period. You need to prioritize over your family holiday or perhaps consider bringing them too. For example, places like Chamonix are great places for the family too.

The best value for money and learning experience may be to join a group course, which is offered by various companies. Alternatively, you could hire a Private Guide. I have used both options and satisfied. You also need to consider the Time Efficiency. For example, if you find a course in Nepal, it will likely include considerable travel time to get actually to the start point of the Training and return. In Europe, Scottish Winter Courses or European Alps. Similarly, in North America and Canada, there are plenty of Course options. In North Asia including Nepal, it is much more difficult to find such courses, with New Zealand offering the best course options in the Southern Hemisphere.

I have also done 5-day trips with a Guide doing Winter Climbing in Scotland around, for example, Ben Nevis Region, one of my favorite places in the Winter. This is typically considerably lower cost then Chamonix. The "Apres Ski" in Ben Nevis is more local Ale and fish n chips, rather than Cheese Fondue and Chardonnay, both equally satisfying.

Bottom line is that its "all-good", get as much time with "boots on the ground" in an Alpine environment as you can practically manage.

What Technical Climbing skills do I need?

99% of the technical skills that you will need and experience above BC is called, Walking, the ability to put one foot in front of the other - not technical climbing. What is important is that you practice the simple practical mountaineering skills and ability to move/walk on mixed terrain, including wearing your mountaineering clothing and using the personal mountaineering equipment that you will use beyond BC. A lot of practical skills with your personal equipment, you can practice at home, and not necessarily need a mountain.

Apart from the Ice Fall, Everest consists of long, sometimes steep snow and ice slopes with short sections of very steep snow/ice or rock climbing (but manageable with 8000m boots and crampons). A reasonably proficient all-around alpine climbing ability is preferred. In addition, the ability for you to do mixed terrain movement and efficient movement on snow and ice including limited rock sections is important.

Secondly, to **practice both Rappelling and forward facing Arm-Wrapping for going downhill both under control** (and to a lesser extent Abseiling). Learn how to loop the rope thru caribiner so that it will brake your descent when for example doing forward descent. Vertical-wall Ice Climbing is not mandatory, but it is useful to have some experience in what this feels like to front-point and the technique (you do not need this on Lhotse Face or elsewhere).

However, I would like to re-emphasise, don't get complacent on Mt Everest, its when you are slack on your basic mountaineering skills when an accident happens e.g. not clipping-in to the line when going thru Ice Fall, not wearing a helmet, poor foot placement, not wearing your glasses and so forth. **It is critical that your caribiner is attached to the rope at all times, via your short safaty line, whether ascending or descending.**

There are relatively small sections where you will be required to clamber up Rock Walls, including specifically on the Summit night. These are obstacles, but remember it's not serious Rock Climbing or Ice Wall front-point Climbing, and you are wearing 8000m Boots, there are foot placements and so forth. It is therefore beneficial to practice ascending and descending steep mixed rock, snow, ice sections with rope and wearing your clothing and personal gear. This doesn't need to be at high altitude, in fact, preferable at low altitude so you can practice, repeat and repeat again. Scotland, European Alps or other similar locations have this type of terrain.

The primary skills that you can practice more before arrival shouls as a minimum include:
- Putting your Harness and Crampons on – critical! Yes, this needs to be said and you should practice whilst wearing your boots and down jacket/suit also. These are critical items of equipment/clothing and when you are on the mountain, in the dark and cold, wearing your gear, it becomes harder. Putting Crampons on will become very exhausting and you really do need to fully tighten the straps. You will be surprised when your Sherpa manages to tighten further then you did…
- Use the Figure-8 with rope i.e. rapelling
- Using the Carabiners (ascend and descending) on the fixed ropes
- Jumar - simple, the issue is more about putting the rope on/off. Remember you always need to be connected to the line. So when you reach an anchor point, clip your safety carabiner to the other side of the anchor point first and then remove your Jumar. This sounds simple, if you don't, then you are not connected and could

simply fall, particularly critical on the Lhotse Face and other upper sections where Jumar is used.
- Mixed Terrain movement on snow/rock/ice, including ascending and descending. The descending movement you shoud get practice since you will be spending many hours and days descending.
- Walking; there are different technical styles, French, German, American etc ! I feel that variations of the French-Step (Penguin style) are more likely to be used, compared to the American "cross-over". Also, walking down-hill, try the "John Wayne" style, wide steps with something dangling between your legs!
- Rapelling, not vertical. Facing both Forward and Backward. For example, from Balcony to C4, C4 to C3 and C3 to bottom of Lhotse Face primarily.
- Arm-wrapping / rappelling. There will be long sections e.g. Summit to C4, Lhotse Face descent, where it will not be steep enough to rappell, but require you to control your descent with the rope. Much of the time you will be walking, facing downwards. Learn to descend reasonably steep angle with the rope wrapped around your forearm and equally through the caribiner for added resistance on the rope. Practice this with the rope wrapped around your arm behind you and in front and what works best for you.
- Abseiling, a handful of sections mostly between C1 and C2. Be confident "going over the edge".
- Ice Axe, minimal or no usage. This may be a surprise, however you may be told that you dont need to bring the ice axe beyond BC.
- Ladder Training (optional)
- Emergency self-arrest procedures i.e. when you fall/slip. You wont know when you are about to slip, so your reaction time and response needs to be immediate and practised.

How important is it to have climbed 7,000m or 8,000m previously?
I recommend it. It is certainly beneficial to have climbed to 7000m+ in my opinion, at least for peace of mind and confidence. I don't believe 8,000m is essential, but nice to have done. Again, it's not mandatory, but will psychologically enable you to know you have been to this altitude already, no unknowns, one less thing to worry about. I certainly believe your body and mind "learns" what it feels like to get to 7,000m+, the sensory inputs, the good and bad feelings and how to reach these altitudes.

In summary, in terms of altitude experience:
- 6,000m+, mandatory
- 7,000m+, recommended
- 8,000m+, preferable but not essential

I recommend that ideally, you spend more time at altitude during the 3 months prior to your departure doing one or two, 5000 – 6000m Peaks, which may take a week.

All the body metrics that you are used to at sea-level may be turned upside down at high altitude and confuse you, particularly during acclimatisation phase. Your heart rate and breathing will increase, whilst your max heart rate, VO2 max and heart stroke volume will decrease. This reduces the amount of blood the heart can pump around the body and therefore less oxygen to muscles. <u>By the time you reach the Summit your VO2 max will be only 20% of the VO2 max at sea level, hence why it becomes a mental battle to overcome the</u>

confusion and exhaustion, rather then relying on your perceived physical fitness. Furthermore, there is already less oxygen in the red blood cells at altitude. You see the challenge. This points to a need for low-intensity training to building your base-fitness and a low-intensity pace whilst on the Mountain to improve acclimatisation. Perhaps the total exhaustion you will be feeling regardless as to whether you are a super-fit athlete, points to the importance of your Mental Strength, which I suggest may "trump" your fitness. This is another reason why prior experience at altitude is beneficial. If you have alternate, relevant experience to an 8000m Peak this may be considered acceptable e.g. Mt Mustagata, Mt Baruntse for example

There is also very much a psychological benefit. If you have been to say 7,000m then you are more likely to reach this altitude on Mt Everest on your Summit Expedition with less mental (and physical) difficulty. You will feel more confident about going to 8,000m. However, if your highest previous altitude is say 6,000m, when you reach 7,000m, you may say to yourself, "that's it, I will turn around now". You stop because of a lack of experience at altitude.

Hypoxic Training/Tent at home or fitness centre. I have known a couple of Mt Everest climbers who have used this approach at home and strongly advocate the benefits (and they Summitted). They certainly performed well, appeared fit and strong and reached the Summit. Whilst there is limited scientific evidence to support the claimed benefits, it is well documented that various Sports Teams and Athletes do high-altitude training camps i.e. with lower Oxygen levels, typically in South America, prior to their competitions.

Mt Everest Camp 3 Training Climb (7200m+)

I strongly recommend you consider this and I completed this successfully in 2017 (and started Camp 3 Training Climb in 2014).

In recent years several Expedition Companies have offered this Expedition. It typically lasts 30 days, costs about USD12,000 and you are part of the Everest and Lhotse Summit Teams going on the same route.

There is no other Expedition that will show you what it feels like to be on Mt Everest then obviously going to C3 on Mt Everest. The benefits are various

- prove to yourself that you can make it, including "knocking-on the head" the infamous Ice Fall, Western Cwm and Lhotse Face (these will no longer be scary unknowns).
- reduce doubts about your ability or identify areas for improvement
- reduce concerns about the unknowns
- you know what training and preparation you need
- you know what worked for you and what didn't, what clothing, gear, food etc
- mental strength and calmness - critical
- help your decision making as to whether to sign-up for the Summit Expedition

Once I decided to sign-up for the Summit Expedition in October 2017, some 6 months after returning from Camp 3 Training Climb I had total Belief and zen-calmness about going for the Summit Expedition – I had little doubt. This is Belief and Confidence based upon Facts, not Delusional thoughts. There were considerably fewer concerns or unknowns in my mind, except from route to C4 and Summit. It is not mandatory and you can certainly Summit Mt

Everest without having completed, however, my view is to reduce uncertainties and this forms part of proper preparation.

Other training points:
Practice wearing your high-altitude clothing / personal equipment
You need to practice with the clothing you will be wearing on the Mountain, particularly the high-altitude clothing and personal equipment. For example, try wearing 8,000m Mitt (and also with 8,000m Glove) with inner liner glove and try:
- Clip-in / out of the line with your carabiner i.e. safety line
- On/off your Jumar on the line, especially at anchor points.
- Do any task! Opening a backpack, having a drink etc

This is very challenging for most people and critical task that you will use constantly. You need to choose your Mitts/Gloves carefully and ideally need finger dexterity, be able to feel your thumb and finger thru the Mitt/Glove. Practice in the shop together when you purchase with a carabiner, jumar etc. Personally, I would remove my 8,000m Mitt and wearing my inner liner glove do the tasks, including on the Summit Day. It is critical that your Mitts and Gloves have the line to attach to your wrists, to prevent dropping them (which is game-over).

For myself, I frequently removed my 8,000m mitts and with my liner gloves changed the Carabiner and Jumar. This is not ideal and risky, but I found it very difficult to achieve the necessary dexterity with the Mitts on. Don't buy Mitts/Gloves that are too large and Practice. Fortunately my hands generally do not get too cold.

Self Sufficiency.
You need to be able to reasonably look after yourself, in terms of your personal admin and movement between Camps, with minimal support or supervision. You need to be able to manage a bad weather situation or storm, either whilst moving or sitting-out in your tent, such that you can return safely. Worst case, you need to be able to move alone, can you imagine descending from C4 to C3 alone? Moving by yourself in a terrain you are not familiar with is as much about your mental state, ability to control your fear, stay calm and think rationally.

Train in poor weather (cold, white-out, wind, snow and so forth).
Practice using your equipment, adjusting your clothing in poor weather. Know what this feels like so you are less surprised on Everest. Preferably this training experience should be in a relatively safer mountain environment, perhaps at a lower altitude and more accessible mountain range.

Is there benefit to hiking during the night, from dusk to dawn? The benefit is that you experience the dark and using your head torch. Perhaps more importantly is the feeling of hiking over hills when you want to sleep and feel tired. The Ice Fall and Summit Night will be the two times on Mt Everest when you are moving thru the night. I recommend trying night hiking once or twice.

Breathing Technique.
How effectively you breath is critical to your performance and efficiency of energy usage and it also acts as a feedback loop i.e. if breathing too hard, then slow down.

There are different techniques, however, the technique I used is Pressure Breathing and Deep, Belly Breathing. Simply, take a Deep inhalation to fill-up more than your typical breath lung and then 4 or more powerful short breathes out in quick succession. Feel the air fill more of your lungs. This is about getting oxygen to more blood cells/capillaries and blood circulation. This pressure breathing is more effective on the incline, but can equally be applied on the Trek into BC

Rest Step
Whilst going uphill, I recommend a technique call the Rest Step. This is an efficient form of slow walking on an incline. This takes practice and steps are also good to practice on. It reduces muscle strain in your thighs. Typically we walk uphill with our legs never fully extended, rather always a 45-degree angle which effectively means the thigh muscle under constant strain and lacks rest. The rest-step makes us fully extend or straighten each leg, so we are effectively standing upright, resting, before moving the next leg. In addition, when moving and extended the leg straight to the vertical, we breath out. We breathe in when we are at the rest phase in between steps. Others may go all-out, faster and stop for rest after 10 steps, vs slower rest-step approach which should enable a more constant and energy efficient movement.

11. Training your Mind and Brain – hand-in-hand with the Body

The biggest challenge in reaching the Summit of Mt Everest is likely to be the Mental one and not giving up, despite how you are feeling, rather then your Physical Fitness or Technical Skills. Your Mind has the words "I will Summit Mt Everest" or "I cannot Summit Mt Everest", you need the former. Be Positive and Stay Positive, despite the low-points.

Firstly, ask yourself Why do you want to Summit Mt Everest? What is your Motivation? How badly do you want it? What motivates you will also drive your actions, training and ultimately the success or otherwise. Remember there are many highly motivated (dead) people on Mt Everest – you don't want to be one of them. Being highly motivated by itself is not enough without adequate experience and training. If you are doing Everest to prove to yourself Whom you are, then perhaps you may wish to try a less risky mountain first. You should choose to climb Mt Everest for Yourself, not anybody else, not family, friends or peers. You should set goals for yourself, what you want to achieve and How you want to achieve your goals, not necessarily how anybody else intends to achieve their goals. We are all different in this regard, don't put yourself into someone else's box.

When the going gets tough you need to keep going, remember you are doing it for your own selfish needs and ego now, nobody else. You need to be able to push to what you think is your limit and maybe beyond it. As you progress in your day you will inevitably get more tired and drained. However do not worry, the Mountain will provide you with renewed Energy and exhilarating Views as you reach new daily goals, that will recharge you!

In my view, your Brain and Mind are just as important to your actions as your legs, heart, and lungs – its a total System with all the sub-components interfaced together and which have a relationship with each other. Your mind, your emotions, your cognition, your thought processes will, in fact, have a corresponding bodily function. Equally, your body controls your brains actions and vice-versa. Learn this relationship and harness it to drive you up the hill, like a Battle Tank in low gear.

Your brain will accept sensory inputs, for example, the mountain conditions e.g. weather and how your body is feeling e.g. exhausted and then determine What is the consequence, the result of how these two parts of the equation add-up at any given point in time, constantly re-evaluating and adapting. The mountain is "living" and constantly changing over 2 months, you as the Mountaineer need to constantly Adapt accordingly to the environment. This process is happening continuously, almost automatically in your sub-conscious without you needing to think about this, the brain is learning from this experience and all your previous mountaineering experiences. It would, therefore, be better to have more mountaineering learning experiences to add to your Mountaineering Body of Knowledge.

Unlike your leg muscles and other bodily functions, your brain is operating 24/7 and much of its function is in the sub-conscious. You are storing many thoughts and learning experiences, that you don't need to consciously think about e.g. how to cross a ladder, how to clip-in to the line. When called upon your brain is looking-up what it previously learned to do in a situation and the resulting action.

You will be feeling many emotions over 2 months and at specific "challenge points" on each day, particularly beyond BC. Emotions are "Hot", immediate and will result in bodily changes, they will direct your immediate physical actions and what you do next. In contrast, rationale reasoned thinking is slower and more tentative. Your brains cognitive processes are more logical. Learn to harness both at the same time and "tame the beast", be ready to go full-force when you need to, when its "Green On, Go!", make sure you make the right decision and act.

The emotion of Fear and harnessing it:
- Fear is but one emotion, albeit perhaps the most powerful emotion you will be feeling and one that you may be feeling very often
- Fear is good, but too little is Risky, too much can be Paralyzing and stop you e.g. the Ladders or the Summit ridge-line (even stop you joining the Expedition).
- So, Embrace Fear, Respect it and Use it.
- You need to lift your head, face fear, knee-it in the nuts then head-butt it and move forward
- Every step you should be aware, appreciate your surroundings, what risks, self-check yourself, not be complacent, even until the very last time thru the Ice-Fall as you walk into Base Camp for the last time.

Don't "psych yourself out" before actually arriving at the "challenge point", don't give in to that fear of the impending unknown. This applies to many sections of the mountain, for example, the Ice Fall, the Lhotse Face, the Summit Cornice Ridge Line and so forth...

Your Emotions will have a tendency to take over your more logical, reasoned, rational thinking processes and you will no doubt get that adrenalin rush or feel stressed that will also release steroids that will impact negatively your memory and risk-management decision-making processes. It is important to control the immediate emotional response to a situation because it may be paralyzing and stop you taking physical action to get out of a dangerous situation. You need to have self-control in your decision making, not let your emotions run wild.

You will need the "yin and yang", to balance your emotions with rational decision making. Your emotions are inputs to your decision making and choosing the next immediate actions, and of course, your emotions may result in a good or bad decision being made. When we are in a stressful, dangerous situation, dark-humour is well understood to be one approach that can be applied. A good example is the military where soldiers "joke" about the deadly nature of their position facing the enemy. You need to try and maintain a sense of humor and a "cool", chilled, mellow outlook...

The Constant Beginner Mindset.
I want to start with good news for you, if you choose to, then the Beginner has the opportunity to have a mindset that will greatly help you achieve a successful Summit whilst managing your risk. It also ties together many of the concepts in this guide. Alternately you can go forward and be the wrong type of Beginner attempting Mt Everest – ignorant, stupid and arrogant, thinking you can Summit without putting in the time and effort.

There is a concept in Zen, that simply put says, the Beginners mind is open, ready to learn despite many years of experience and training. Their mind is open to many possibilities, open to asking questions, no pre-conceived answers. By contrast, the more experienced, so-called professional or expert mountaineers mind is often closed and they are arrogant.

A Beginner is not arrogant, he is humble, has humility and ready to learn from the Master – in this case, Mt Everest.

A Beginner is cautious and careful but has boldness and bravery to move forward, to learn, to suffer.

This concept applies whether you are an actual beginner or a more experienced Mountaineer

Practical Training Points

Calm yourself. You will be in a constant state of extreme Exhaustion beyond BC, struggle to put one foot in front of another and like a flat battery wanting to stop. You will be very confused How and Why is this happening. The reality is that your VO2 Max is about 20% compared to Sea Level. You can make it. Its a matter of pace and being able to go for several hours simply by step-by-step. Try and calm your mind from the confusion and negative signals your brain is receiving.

Mental Strength. If you are a marathon Runner and decide its too hard you can stop, get a bus and go home. Unfortunately, Mt Everest does not allow us to do that. When we are at the point of total failure you cannot simply give up at Camp 3 and be teleported home. You need to find the strength to keep going.

Draw on past Experience. That's one good reason to Train hard and get mountain experience prior so you know what this feels like and how to get thru it. Reduce the Unknowns.

"Mental Wall" to negative thoughts. At many points in time over the 2 months, your Brain will be constantly receiving signals telling it "Why am I here, I should not be here", "I am scared". You will hear the Avalanches constantly at BC, stare at the tumbling Ice Fall or maybe the seemingly vertical Lhotse Face. You need to block these dark thoughts, build a mental Wall as if you are tone-deaf, focus on having a Positive mind-set

"Get on with it". You will see and hear Everest for 2 months. It will have a psychological impact on you, especially at BC admiring the Ice Wall and sounds of avalanches all around you 24/7. You will have nerves about what's coming. Best thing is to "Get On With It", don't brood and you will be amazed afterward. The next time will be much less worrying (and hopefully stronger too)

Goals. Mt Everest and other high altitude mountains are perfect for breaking-down a Goal into smaller goals that are more manageable and enable a mental plan or model to be prepared.

Making a Plan (and "binning the Plan"). You should make a Plan of the different sections of the mountain, the specific obstacles overcome and so forth and this will be stored in your memory, so in fact, when you are moving on the mountain you are in fact using a past plan from your memory. The problem is that "no plan survives contact with the enemy", in this context, the Mountain. The challenge with Mt Everest is Mother Nature and the large number of Objective Risks that are not 100% predictable based on your Plan. Again, adaptation, flexibility, open-mind is as important as a good plan. You need to be ready to change your plan very quickly. If you have a fixed view then you are more likely to fail then being open-minded and agile to the changing situation and ultimately succeed.

The Mental Model of the Route. If you have planned the route in your mind and consciously walked thru each step or action in your mind beforehand then you are likely to have a higher probability of achieving that particular goal. You are in fact making a model of future success.

How can I make a mental model of the plan, the route from Camp 2 to Camp 3 if it's my first time? The answer is simple, do the Training Climb to Camp 3 – I hope I am emphasizing the importance.

12. Your fellow Climbers – the "team dynamic"

Learn to get along and support each other - its only 2 months. However if it doesn't work out, then take a breath, be calm, go to your tent for a break. Remember if the team fractures and people spinout and loose it emotionally, it may jeopardize the entire team Summit goal.

Put yourself in the mind-set of your team members. Each person will have ups/downs, be stronger/weaker and feel different emotionally about different situations at different times over the 2 months.

When you are in your Dining Tent or talking at BC, perhaps as a Beginner its better to listen and listen to the people with the experience, not those in the team whom talk a lot and are so called "experts", "walking Encyclopedias" but have never summited the Mountain yet.

Whilst it is impressive that there are several hundred people at Base Camp whom have the same unified goal, drive, desire (and concerns) to reach the Summit, **the irony is that it is these same fellow climbers that are likely to become one of the major challenges and risks to you on the Mountain and especially on your final Summit push**, from C4 to Summit and descent i.e. creating a bottle-neck. Perhaps the only way to mitigate this risk is to avoid the crowds, the line of climbers on the final ridge-line and therefore climb later in the Summit window / week (or possibly the first day, however likely to be more climbers then at the end of the Summit window and therefore I prefer later)

Teams are normally about Trust and Confidence in each other and liking the people you are with which is normally built over time. You need to understand that this is generally not the case in a typical commercial Expedition where people are thrown together in the grinder for 2 months

Lets consider your individual unit. Let's be harsh and perhaps honest, understand this is not a "real Team", rather a group of individuals with similar personalities, selfish, egotistical goals that are forced together in a hostile, pressure-cooker environment with the goal to Summit Mt Everest. This is not a Team in the military context that has been tested, trained and lived together, that knows each other and so forth. Not everyone in your team and those climbers around you has the same technical ability and standard, hence the variables and risks are varying constantly and your success is partially dependent on others – they are part of the Summit Success Equation. You will not likely know each other but will need to live together on an amazingly hard challenge that will have both ups and downs, success and failure, including possible injury, medical situations and worse.

The reality is that this expedition is largely dependent upon your individual effort rather than a team effort to get you to the next Camp (whilst fully appreciating the Sherpa support, tent set-up and so forth). Whilst it will take an individual effort, your success will also depend on others, most notably the Sherpa's and your Personal Sherpa whom will / should be at or near your side on the Summit-push. You also need your teammates for companionship, to talk too and share the daily struggles and have a joke together. Equally, you don't 100% need the team or persons next to you to progress up or down, so can try to reduce contact with a person(s) that you may not get along with. The real test of the group dynamic will come if there is an "emergency situation". The reality is that if a situation happens to one of the team, then that will have a direct impact or consequence to the others in the team, in terms of their plans and movement up/down the mountain – it is a System. You are in a group but it's all about you as the individual ultimately.

During the 2 months, particularly after you arrive at BC, there will inevitably be various issues, debates, tensions that come up from the minor to the more important. Ultimately you need to do what is right for you and not be "bullied" by others or "group think".

Understand that Expedition Company is a commercial enterprise, whose goals are to minimize risk and allow you to achieve your goal but at the same time be financially Profitable and have Repeat Clients. Mt Everest is big – Big business and there are many different stakeholders trying to capitalize, some less scrupulously.

Understand that Sherpa's are hard, albeit mostly jovial people, doing a hard Job, they are not there to necessarily be your friend and read you bedtime stories - it is a risky and hard job for which they are well paid, in the Nepal context. Equally, not all Sherpa's are created equal and there are differences between them, just like all of us. The key is to sync with Sherpa's that you get along with and hopefully a Personal Sherpa that syncs with you, your strengths and weaknesses.

No surprises amongst the hardest working people are the humble Porters, whom are the lowest paid and have literally backbreaking work. Be kind and generous.

13. Personal Risk Management - The Risks and How to reduce

You should realize this book is all about managing risk and you need to take personal responsibility for managing your own risk, and not be completely reliant on others i.e. your Leader, your Sherpa's, your Teammates, whom in reality will not be "holding your hand" all the way up and down. Some of the Risks you can work to mitigate or reduce and actually improve your Odds.

If you like risk and the adrenalin attract adventure and mountaineering then part of you, but that should not mean you want to take a risk too far. The Risk is also a magnet and is also part of the reason you are attracted to Mt Everest. All Mountaineers are risk managers and you should constantly evaluate the risk, and you will do this almost sub-consciously as you gain more experience in the mountains – you will gain a "sixth-sense" or "gut feeling". For every situation or Action there is a Consequence e.g. if I stay in the "popcorn field" in the Ice Fall, what is the probability that a rock may hit me. You need to apply a Personal Risk Management Approach.

Theoretically, you need to understand the Threat and what is the Residual Risk after applying your Risk Mitigation (remember I do Risk Management as part of my day-job). Applying a Common-Sense approach that is rational and objective is often the best approach but in a worst-case scenario, this goes hand-in-hand with what's in your Heart, in terms of whether you will survive. Most importantly is that you return home, whether you Summit or not. You need to decide how much risk you can accept. Each person will have a different risk appetite and depends on each person's perspective and assessment of the same situation.

The fundamental risk as a Beginner that you face on Mt Everest is that the difficulties, challenges, and threats you will face are exactly the same as the Professional, expert Mountaineer. The Mountain does not care and conveniently adjust the risk level since you are a Beginner - sorry.

Risk Strategy and "worst case" management – preparation
You need to plan for the worst and hope for the best. You need to walk thru in your mind what are the scenarios and what do you need to prepare to get out of the situation. Equally, do not become paranoid with trying to be 100% safe, since its fatalistic and impossible to guarantee. You need to be honest, accepting of risks that you are going to face.

The paradox of taking risks to reduce risks. In order to succeed on Mt Everest you need to have been "burned" and learned hard, painful lessons – actually taken risks. You need to experience these risks on other more "safer" Mountains, or with a Guide, in order to have these learning takeaways that will be hard-wired into your mind for Mt Everest. Stress and risk are good for learning, in a safer, controlled environment and in moderation. This could be described as a feedback loop, taking Risks increasing Learning and in a constant loop cycle. Of course, this can get to the point where you take more and more risks and then the system breaks, suddenly, when you don't expect it and you fall off the mountain face – this is Mother Nature, not a Risk Spreadsheet. There are many stories of famous, world-class Mountaineers whom didn't "beat the clock" and took one too many risks.

The Correct Experience to Reduce Risk
You need to get the right type of "good" experience specifically for Mt Everest in order to take the correct action. How you assess risk is equally about how you Perceive what's happening around you. How you personally see yourself and situation at any point in time. Each person perception of risk will be different. You may have plenty of bad experience and poor technique on the mountain, but not realize it, until it is too late. You may be in fact fooling yourself accordingly. Ironically, it may, therefore, be your experience rather than your lack of experience that becomes a reason for an accident – you have become complacent. You may be arrogant or ignorant to the risks of Mt Everest and be fooled into thinking your past experience is good enough. You also need to understand that risk is a system and that risk is compounded by the inter-linkages of the parts of the system. For example, if you are roped-together in what seems a more safe arrangement if the person at the top falls then you are also likely to be dragged off the mountain also. When you face a stressful and clearly risky situation, your pulse rate will increase, adrenalin will flow, your body and hands may start shaking and you may not be able to understand the situation clearly and take the correct action. Again, if you have gained Experience in such situations or trained in the Mountains then you are more likely to be able to stay calm and think clearly. This experience will also help you to adapt to the situation rapidly.

Action is the Key.
Whether you are experienced or not, you are likely to feel emotions and fear. Your Expertise and your Emotions are equally important to get out of the situation and reasoning is required to manage those emotions to your benefit. The key point is when you are in a situation What Action do you do Next? The point is not to become paralyzed and do nothing, you need to face the reality of the situation and assess the course of Action in a timely manner. For example, if you are on the Summit ridge-line and their is a bottle-neck you cant sit down, freeze and fall asleep.

Extracting yourself quickly or "Sitting-out" may be the right course of Action but think thru the Options before you decide. Stop, Think, Plan and Act.

"Shock Action".
Accidents often happen as a result of what are often illogical actions and poor decision making. The emotions and reasoning are not balanced. You may be Confused due to various factors and make poor decisions or actions. At that critical point, you need to have that shock impulse to "stand-up in the storm" and get down the mountain. You may be on your own, do you have the confidence to be self-reliant and move without anyone with you?

You may feel that its all your past experience, training and mountaineering equipment that will enable you to survive life-threatening situations on the Mountain but in reality its likely to be more about your Heart at that critical, life-threatening point.

All mountain experiences we have will contribute to your Mountaineering Body of Knowledge that you can call upon sub-consciously to make better decisions and take necessary Action.

Practical Risk issues on the Mountain
- Dont be a heroic "tough guy". Dont think you can "conquer the Mountain" or "beat the Weather" – you can't and Mt Everest doesnt care. Dont imagine you can leave your tent, regardless of the weather conditions and battle thru bad-weather at any

point on the Mountian especially on the Summit-push. **When you are on the Summit dont hang-around and hope to be the last person to leave the Summit – the weather may change or a bottle-neck of people may result increasing the risks considerably**. You need to reach the Summit and expeditiously get down to the relative safety of C4.
- There will be a lot of Emotion flying around, coupled with High Altitude Weather and tough Mountain Conditions. Your emotions are important "hot and immediate" sensory inputs to your brain. They are important in terms of managing Risk. Understand the emotion and how to translate it into an appropriate physical action.
- Simply, there are Objective Risks relating to the Mountain conditions and Personal Risks, the latter relating to your own situation. Objective Risks relate to the Mountain Conditions and the Weather primarily. These Risks are difficult to manage and the best way to mitigate these risks is not to be in the threat location i.e. avalanche zone. So, for example, stay in the tent, go lower, get off the Mountain, depending on the situation!
- There is also what I consider a Third major risk category – your fellow climbers, both in your team and all the other Expeditions. Specifically, they may result in bottle-necks at critical locations i.e. Summit night. Everyone will have different levels of skill and experience and may be in better or worse condition at any given point/location on the Summit-push.
- Playing Russian Roulette or a Game of Chess with the Mountain. You are making a series of moves on the mountain over 2 months, equally, the mountain is making its moves, expect the mountain is Mother Nature and its moves are not necessarily logical or reasoned, rather many random events that happen at great speed with devasting effect. The Mountain is in a constant state of change, it is dynamic, but you may not realize these changes are happening and not adjust your game-plan. At a given point on the mountain facing difficulties, there is a real potential that risks are in fact compounding, stress, tension, exhaustion, altitude illness, deteriorating weather. At the same time, your ability to think rationally is decreasing. You need to have a pre-prepared Exit Plan. If in doubt, Go Down.
- Medical problems, from AMS to being hit by a rock, are often the result of a Threat not being understood, assessing the actual Risk that it poses and how to Mitigate this Risk. For example, don't delay in Ice Fall, don't rest in the "popcorn field" where you see fallen small rocks all around you, don't walk adjacent the face of Nuptse from C1 to C2
- Be Rational and Objective. If in doubt, Stop, Think, Plan, Act and Go Down (safely). Risks are often about personal Perception and each person may take a different view on the Risk.
- In Path Finding in any terrain, a good technique is to Turn Around and look at your route as if you were descending. Make a mental map or snap-shot in your memory of the key points/obstacles on the route. This may be more important is you have near white-out conditions.
- Don't make impulsive decisions or behavior that cause you to make the wrong decision
- You need to know your personal equipment and equally the System and forces that is the mountain.
- Listen to others, especially those with Experience. This applies more so the higher up you go, particularly on the Summit Night.
- Train Hard to mitigate Risks (or be very lucky). We have spoken about Training in other sections of this Guide, however training to mitigate risks is equally valid. As I

have suggested, managing your emotions is critical to risk management, in addition to your Technical and Brain Training.

Examples that have happened to me on expeditions are below, some down to my own errors and making simple mistakes. Note it is these simple but potentially serious, painful mistakes that ensure we don't make the same mistake twice.
- Equipment Failure - Heels detaching from Boots in Ice-Fall, Mt Everest 2017.
- Altitude Sickness - irrational thinking near Summit Aconcagua and Summit Baruntse. Perhaps poor acclimatization or too fast in case of Mt Aconcagua.
- Snow Blindness – On the day before leaving Mt Mustagata I forgot to wear my Glacier Glasses at Base Camp. This will be like sand in your eyes and typically last 24 – 48 hours, gradually improving. Very little treatment, warm green-tea bags and keep covered). I remember arriving at Kashgar at midnight and the bright neon lights of our hotel garden as we celebrated thru my bandana covered eyes.
- Serious Sun-Burn – summit day to Mt Mustagata, I forgot to apply my sun-cream and half my face was deeply burned as the Sun rose to my right side.
- Banged-up Ribs - On repelling from C3 to C2 I slipped during a repel going over a short steeper section. This took several months to recover fully and was painful to move and sleep. No treatment.
- Hemeroids (twice). The last time was in Namche on the way-out, after we had Summitted. I won't describe the graphic details, but I did consider an Insurance Helicopter Rescue since I could not easily walk (I did, in fact, hire a Helicopter with 3 others to KTM). You can also buy cream in Namche Pharmacies

Accidents
The most common factors on Mt Everest when accidents are likely to include the following:
- Descending (you slip)
- Roped together (less likely on Mt Everest unless needed)
- No fixed protection (you have not clipped-in)

Other accidents and particularly Objective Risks can include Crevasse fall, Avalanche, Ice-Fall collapse and being hit by rocks/objects. External factors like bad-weather and bottle-neck's I dont necessarily classify as an accident, more a risk, but may result in accident happening.

Let's consider Descending, say from the Summit.
Most deaths occur between C4 – Summit – C4.
The temperature before Sunrise may drop to -40c or below. Wind-chill and standing still will rapidly lower your body temperature and freeze you – try to not be stationary for very long, although I accept this may be difficult if a bottle-neck on the ridge-line. If you are stationary you will freeze, your oxygen will finish and you may die.

If you are Sleepy and sit down/lean against ridge to rest you may not wake up – try to avoid "curling into a ball" and sleeping. Also it may be very difficult for your Sherpa to wake you and help you descend.

If White-out conditions then stop, dont walk blindly, you may go off the edge or simply in the wrong direction, especially if confused and for some reason not clipped-in. If your hands and/or feet start getting cold, you start to loose your vision, the wind picks-up, it becomes a white-out your fear levels will inevitably increase. Dont panic – it will not help you. Remember the basics, keep moving but in a safe manner as possible, not recklessly. If your hands and/or feet start getting cold, you start to loose your vision, the wind picks-up, it becomes a white-out your fear levels will inevitably increase. Dont panic – it will not help you. Remember the basics, keep moving but in a safe manner as possible, not recklessly.

You could also slip on the large, relatively steep sections of the slope or one of the rock-steps that you need to descend down. You will be feeling emotions of happiness which is a positive emotion that has resulted in you lowering your guard and you need to be even more alert then going upwards towards the Summit. Unfortunately, you are only half-way and the reality is that the more risky section of the Summit day is on the descent. Let's also consider Stress that is another risk factor. You will be exhausted, thirsty, cold, possibly suffering from the altitude that all contribute to the chance of an accident. Finally, descending is actually more technically difficult and riskier than climbing upwards. You need careful foot placement, moving your body weight carefully and have no Jumar for protection, only your hand to brake your fall. Again, now more then ever, remember to always have your safety line clipped-in. Learn how to use, brake, slow yourself and rappel efficiently.

You must always ensure your safety line/caribiner is clipped-in to the rope at all times at any section of the Mountain, whether ascending or descending and ensure you can slow/stop yourself effectively.

Medical Issues – background – what's happening to your body?
Lets first briefly look at what happens to the body as you go higher since it is important to understand what you will be feeling and why. As you go higher the following happens:
- barometric pressure drops
- air becomes thinner and
- less Oxygen becomes available

If we consider your body and summarise:
- your Heart is the Engine.
- Oxygen is carried around the body in red blood cells in the blood
- the Oxygen is gathered from the atmosphere by the Lungs
- your Heart, Brain, Muscles and so forth need the Oxygen to function. If you don't get sufficient Oxygen then you will slow down, stop or worse.

However, as you gain altitude there is less Oxygen available whilst your workload is the same or increased (herein lies the crux of the difficulty on Everest or other high-altitude Mountains). Therefore your body; increases your breathing rate, increases your heart rate and tries to increase the number of red blood cells carrying the oxygen.

Harder Breathing. As you go higher your breathing will Adapt and you will breath harder and more often. This improves with time at altitude but never achieves the same level as if you were at home. There are different breathing techniques but fundamentally you will breath harder and more often at altitude whether at rest or when moving. The technique that I use is deep, slow, belly-breathing and several pressure breaths out.

Higher Pulse Rate. This will increase, similarly as a result of the need to pump more red blood cells around the body carrying the Oxygen. It is useful to measure at rest, particularly when you wake-up. Some watches can record the last several hours of your pulse rate. My pulse rate was typically 52 whilst sleeping.

Thickening Blood. This will get thicker due to fluid loss and also the need to generate more red blood cells. However, equally your blood may thicken too much and your blood cells may not be able to travel as fast. This thickening of the blood may result in a blood clot This is a worst-case result, which does indeed happen to climbers on high-altitude Peaks, and may result in reduced Oxygen being transported. This can happen regardless of their fitness level and super-fit people are known to have had this problem resulting in expedition being canceled. Anecdotal evidence suggests Exercise and Aspirin are often sighted as potentially helping

Medical Issues - what can go wrong and how to reduce risk - Go Down.
If you are not feeling well then you should seek medical advice from a medical professional. There is a long list of potential medical problems that you will face, some small, some show-stoppers. You will have read with concern, and rightly, about High Altitude Cerebral Edema (HACE), High Altitude Pulmonary Edema (HAPE) or AMS (Acute Mountain Sickness). These are potentially deadly if not identified and managed quickly and effectively. Equally, if you have Frostbite or Snow Blindness above BC then this may dramatically increase your risk level, since your effective movement will be impaired and you may take chances. You will also need to be escorted down the mountain to safety and treatment.

The truth is a relatively small percentage of climbers will suffer from High Altitude Cerebral Edoema (HACE), High Altitude Pulminory Edeoma (HAPE) or AMS. The simple and still most effective advice is Go Down and Go Down Immediately (and safely). If you are diagnosed then I recommend this descent is with someone else who is able to help if your situation worsens enroute, preferably a Sherpa or Deputy Leader. Note, this is where the number of Resources in your team will become apparent and whether a Rescue compromises the Team safety and from moving.

I have personally known two persons on different Expeditions, both attempting Lhotse whom were both diagnosed with HAPE at BC and C1. They descended to Pheriche, where the Hospital is located, and many people including themselves thought their trip may be over. 2 weeks later they returned and went on to Summit, successfully. It's not necessarily over, think positively, but be realistic.

The simplest approach if suffering with any of altitude symptoms is often to Rest in the location or stay overnight. You should certainly not Ascend. If the symptoms persist you should Descend. You should seek medical advice and constantly monitor yourself or make sure others are aware of your symptoms. There are a variety of Drugs and medicines that you can take and I recommend seeking medical advice on what medicines to take.

The reality is that the most common medical issues you are likely to be as follows, and you should work to both primarily prevent (take lozenges, cough medicine daily) and resolve quickly if you succumb, with having enough medication (more then necessary).
- Colds, runny nose,
- A sore Throat, Cough
- High Altitude Cough (worse than "normal" cough) – the infamous "Khumbu cough"
- Headache

- Diarrhea
- Gastric / Stomach Bug

If you are ill with above, then you should think of your fellow climbers and consider effectively quarantining yourself to your tent, especially if at BC. People get nervous, especially when you are having dinner and coughing at the table.

In conclusion, Stay Healthy. This is probably one of the most important battles to fight and equally one of the largest challenges.

Sherpas

- You are unlikely to be able to Summit without Sherpa Power support (and the support team of porters, cooks and so forth)
- A Sherpa cannot drag you to the Summit (and what's the point if they could)
- A Sherpa can, maybe, help you get down. There is no guarantee they can get you down, they seem super-human but they are human and get tired, but can certainly help. You may not be co-operative either thru selfishness, altitude sickness, injury or "Summit-fever". It is therefore important to **make the right decision in good time whilst you are still mentally coherent and physically able to do so – its like an egg-timer running down.** There are many accurate stories of climbers not turning around and subsequencty passing-away due to "Summit fever" or simply not listening to advice of others around them before it was too late – dont be one of those people. Whilst Sherpas are some sort of "Insurance Policy" they are certainly not a guarantee your life will be saved. Sorry.
- A Sherpa can help you avoid pitfalls (literally point out the crevasse, remind you to clip-in), help you with your gear setup, help you carry your personal gear, give advice and opinion, give you confidence, "pat you on the back" (not very often, these are hard people without much Western-style sentiment)
- Sherpas are also typically paid for load-carries, which is why you may see them going up and down from BC

Pace - all Sections

I am strongly of the view that Pace is key to overall success or failure and this very much relates to Acclimatisation also, which is so fundamental. Physical Pace directly impacts your Mental State i.e. good pace and you feel mentally positive/calm. Equally, if you are "blowing-up" then you will feel mentally stressed and start questionning yourself and whether you can make it or decide to give-up. Also, if you perceive yourself as being "last" or slowest person in the team, this will also impact you negatively. This is a state-of-mind, your outlook – adjust it.

You are in a group, but most important is finding your own pace, not others. It's not a race or a competition although it will naturally feel good to be first or make you doubt yourself when you are last. It means nothing. Don't feel too good or bad, the next day may be very different. Climbing Mt Everest and returning safely is a "long game".

You will know if you feel like Vomiting if you have a Headache. You need to listen to your body and mind, how do you feel? Stop, Rest, Think, Adjust. You need to adjust your pace accordingly.

One effective measure of your pace is your pulse rate. For myself, I consciously tried to keep my pulse rate relatively Low and used by Watch to show my pulses its primary display. I endeavored to keep my pulse around the 80+ BPM range, including whilst ascending (of course, sometimes this spikes). I suppose that's about 60% of my maximum. This applied on the Trek to BC, Acclimatisation Hikes and beyond BC upwards. I endeavored to maintain a steady, efficient, "comfortable" pace (I importantly clarify comfortable to mean not overly slow), which I coupled with Breathing Techniques and Rest Step. Other indicators are that you will know if you are "blowing up", pushing too hard and can feel your "heart beating thru your ears".

Rest, calm yourself and enjoy the view. This is as much psychology as practical need to drink, eat and recover. If you are operating at near 100% and want to "rush" then you are increasing your risks and reducing the effectiveness of your decision making, particularly in a risky situation

Cut-Off Times
Acclimatisation Phase.
Some Expedition Companies have cut-off times during the acclimatization phase. If you don't make the cut-off then you are binned prior to being allowed a Summit Push Attempt. Actually, I thought this was harsh, however after having now Summited, I am in agreement with this principle and it's really in your best interests. If you are too slow, then there is a reason behind it and this may compromise both your own and your team members chance of success and increase the risks to all concerned. This doesn't mean its all over, rather you may be given chance to try again or come back another year (or even this season).

It is critical to understand that whilst there is a limited risk of going "slowly" from Lukla to BC, which I recommend, it is equally important to understand that if you take "too long" and "too slow" beyond the BC, then this is an increased risk. It is a matter of assessing Why am I taking a long time i.e. illness, exhaustion. You will be able to tell if you are "too slow":
- am I feeling physically and mentally exhausted?
- am I constantly far behind the others in group pace?
- is the Sherpa / Leader showing overly concern or encouragement?

You need to minimize the time that you spend on the risky sections of the climb. Equally, some people will benefit from staying at C1 and above for a week whilst others may get worse in terms of acclimatization. This is dependent on the individual.

Summit Night
There is no fixed turnaround time, however you should be heading down around 1200 – 1400, regardless of where you are on the mountain, so that you can be in C4 before sunset.

14. Timeline Overview – 2 months

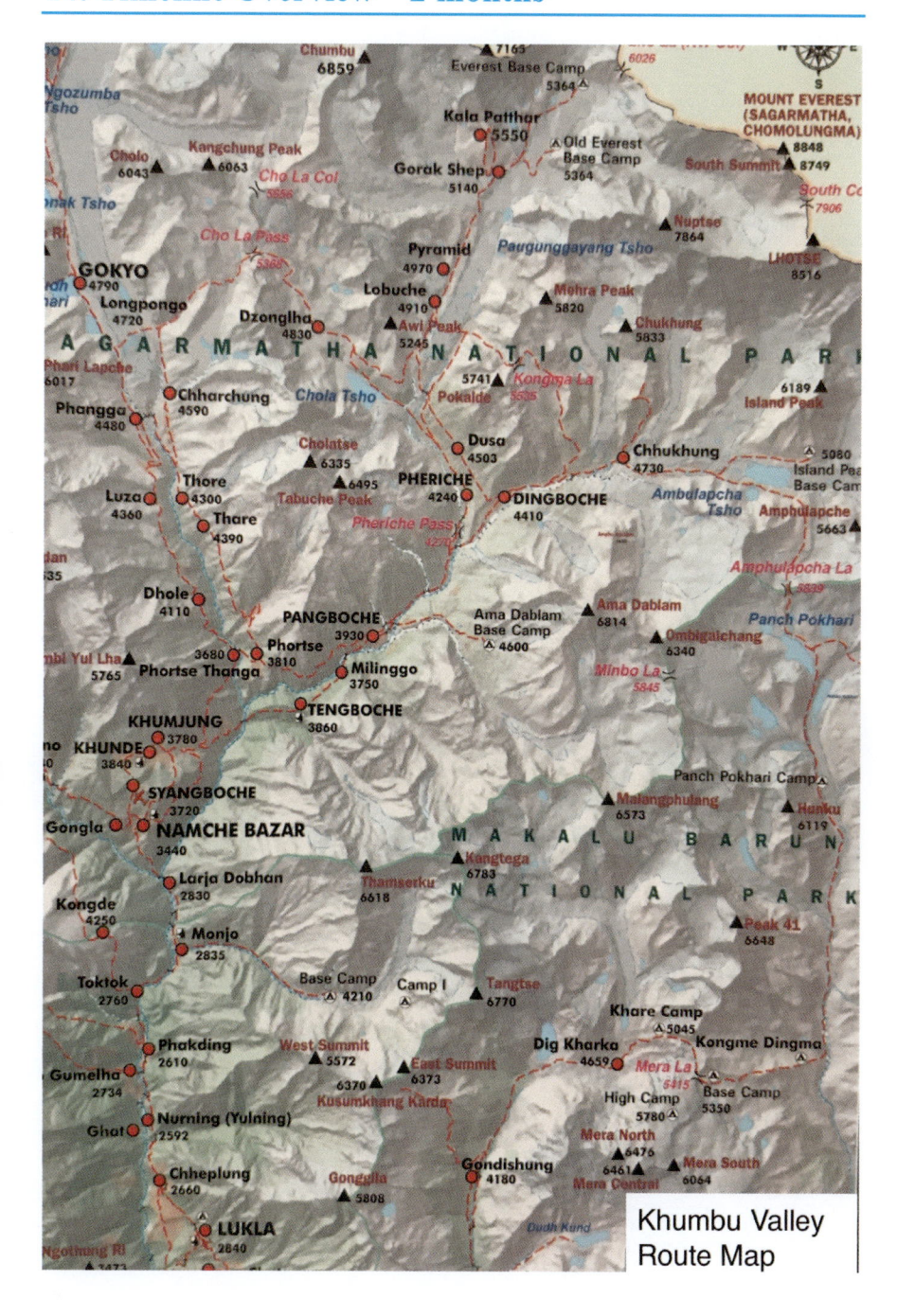

A typical Timeline will take 2 months. However, there are shorter options but for Beginner let's consider the typical. There will be some variations, but most critically when the Summit window opens all teams will be going for it in this window.

Below is a typical Summary of the 8 weeks. There are variations between Expeditions. This schedule is based on two acclimatisation rotations thru the Ice Fall and a final Summit Rotation. On our expedition, we did a single acclimatisation rotation thru the Ice Fall to C3 (and a final Summit Rotation). We spent longer above C1, with more nights at C2. This worked for us but may not work for everyone, particularly if you are suffering or have altitude illness. Remember, at altitude, BC and above, you will struggle to recover from any ailments and may likely get worse. The logic was primarily to reduce time spent in the Ice Fall.

8-Week Overview
1. Week 1 - Kathmandu and Trek into BC
2. Acclimatisation Day-Hikes:
    a. "Everest View Hotel" for morning tea then Khumjung for Sherpa Stew accessed from Namche. It is a very scenic circuit walk to Khumjung.
    b. Chukung Ri 5550m, accessed from Dingboche. This is particularly testing.
    c. Some companies also include Lobuche East Summit en route to BC
3. Week 2 – Arrive at BC. Acclimatisation and Hiking.
    a. Mt Pumori C1 and surrounds is very accessible from BC and you will undertake. At Gorek Shep, Kalar Patar also offers Acclimatisation opportunity.
4. Week 3 - Acclimatisation - BC, C1, C2
5. Week 4 - Rest at BC and easy day-Hiking
6. Week 5 - BC, C1, C2, C3
7. Week 6 - Rest & Recovery Week
8. Week 7 – Summit Week
    a. Day 1 - C1 (optional or push to C2, after rest-stop C1, more commonly
    b. Day 2 - C2
    c. Day 3 - C3
    d. Day 4 - C4
    e. Day 5 – Summit
    f. Day 6 - C4
    g. Day 7 - C2
    h. Day 8 - BC
9. Week 8 – Trek Out / Heli to Katmandu

Elevation (m)

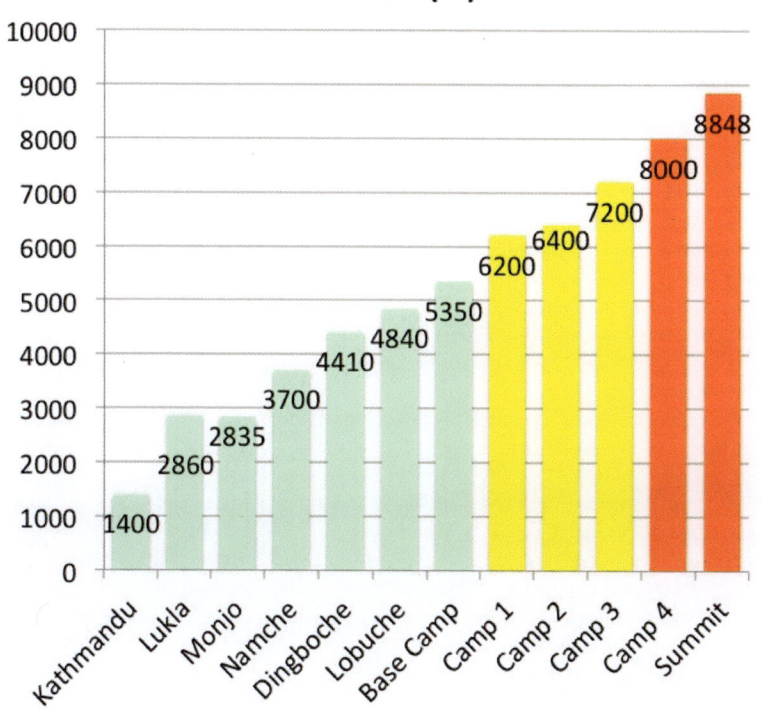

Location	Elevation (m)
Kathmandu	1400
Lukla	2860
Monjo	2835
Namche	3700
Dingboche	4410
Lobuche	4840
Base Camp	5350
Camp 1	6200
Camp 2	6400
Camp 3	7200
Camp 4	8000
Summit	8848

Typical Day Routine
Depending where on the Trek / Mountain you are - do the basics right and diligently
1. Wake-Up. I said a small Prayer to the Mountain, a Prayer to your Spiritual God (you may become a Believer!) and "pat yourself on the back", say "well done". You made it thru the last day and today is a new day. Don't dwell on the past or think too far ahead - focus on today.
2. Personal Admin, Hygiene and any Medicines
3. Drink. Minimum 4 liters per day. Critical. I force down 1 liter immediately upon waking up in the tent/lodge.
    a. I recommend putting sports drink tablet in your water, even when not "active" e.g. at BC or rest days
    b. You will lose more fluids thru respiration then at low altitude and the air is drier.
    c. If you are losing fluid thru sweating then you are wearing too many layers.
4. Eat. Get calories inside you, both team meal and your personal. Your personal food when moving is likely to be Carbo based i.e energy bars, gels and so forth.
5. Suck on minimum 2 throat-lozenge per day, even if you don't have a sore throat. This is critical. Prevention is key.
6. Wear your Buff, especially when moving. Critical.
7. Wear your glasses. Critical
8. Wear your hat. Critical.
9. Put on sunscreen and lip balm.
10. In your Sleeping Bag. Repeat no.1. You made it thru the day!

Week 1 – Kathmandu
Your Expedition Success starts the moment on landing at Kathmandu airport, understand this important point.

Be careful not to get a stomach bug or a sore throat and if you are not used to Nepali/Asian food then perhaps stick to Pizza. Equally, the streets are dusty and dirty.

If you have not got all your personal gear then don't worry, you can certainly rent or purchase whatever extras you may need, from medicines, mountaineering boots to 8,000m clothing. However, be cautious of the fakes in Thamel and there are also legitimate Shops also, including the leading international brands.

Week 2 - Lukla to Base Camp
Relax, Go Slowly, enjoy the view, have a cup of tea and cake enroute.

The Go Slowly is the most important point to note. Your goal should be to be the last person in your team arriving at the next village each day. There is no rush each day to arrive at the next village. It's not a competition with your recently formed team trying to gauge eachothers strength and experience and your position in the group. Dont get pysched out if a team member decides to try and do a maximum number of press-ups in the dining area of the lodge in front of everyone – they may quit by C1. It is more important that you try to arrive feeling reasonably healthy, happy, relaxed and not completely exhausted. What is the point in arriving lunchtime and hanging around till bed-time, twiddling your thumbs?

It is critically important that you try to avoid and prevent any respiratory problems, "Khumbu Cough" and so forth since it will take longer to cure and get worse once at Base Camp – it will impact your performance. Altitude Illness rarely happens suddenly, especially at lower altitudes, and it is during the trekking phase where the acclimatisation phase starts that you are first exposed to the symptoms of altitude illness. Your body will start to acclimatise and therefore expect changes in how you feel. You may feel tired, feel ill, lose appetite, have headaches, can't sleep, high pulse rate and so forth. However, it is important that you assess whether you have any altitude illness symptoms and resolve them. Do not continue upwards if you have symptoms. Seek medical advice, which may include medicines, sleeping an extra night or descending.

I recommend going slowly, talk to your fellow trekkers, to the friendly locals and have a cup of Masala tea or two at the Lodges on the way (this later applies up to Pheriche, after this point it becomes more rugged and less hospitable).

Typical itinerary with minimum days as follows (this can be extended depending on how you feel, don't worry about being a day behind your team members):
1. Lukla 2860m (1 night optional or trek down valley late morning after arrival, 2+ hours)
2. Monjo 2835m (1 night)
3. Namche 3400m (2 nights)
4. Dingboche 4410m or Pheriche (2 night).
5. Lobuche 4940m (1 night)
6. BC 5350m (or optional stay at Gorek Shep, last night in a "bed" !)

Note, there is slack in the Schedule and if you need an extra night along the trail it will not impact the overall Schedule, do not be concerned, despite you being concerned that "falling behind" the Team. It has no impact over a 2-month Schedule, but if you get ill/exhausted on the trekking phase it will impact your expedition later since takes time to get rid of colds and so forth.

For myself, I trekked with my family to Namche, then trekked back to Lukla, so they could catch a flight, then Heli to Namche (USD150) and caught up with the team a day or so later – no impact whatsoever on the Expedition.

Week 3, 4, 5 – refer "The Route – beyond Base Camp to the Summit and Return" below
After you have arrived at BC there will be rest-days. You may consider Away-Day's when at BC i.e. get out from BC. You may get fed up of the surroundings at BC. When you have a couple of days spare in the schedule, then a good option is to spend a night at, for example, Gorek Shep. Benefits:
- lodge with bed and shower
- dining room with better or different menu (especially Sherpa Stew)
- different people
- lower elevation
- better Internet/communications, hopefully
- not stare at the Ice Fall and hear the many Avalanches all around you
- you also get some hiking exercise on each day

Week 6 - Rest & Recovery Week
This is self-explanatory and most important to your Summit success. The last weeks are culminating in the Summit Week, for which you ideally need to be at your Peak Performance.

There are two options, stay at BC or go down Valley. I strongly recommend the later and at the earliest opportunity depart from BC.

I cannot think of any real benefits to staying at BC except saving cash and some may argue "staying in the zone and focussed", I don't agree with the later, although dependent upon the individual. If you stay at BC, you will continue to not sleep properly, not recover, not strengthen your body or mind, not be able to buy Summit Week provisions and not enjoy a pizza down the Valley.

What are the benefits of going down Valley?
In terms of physiological the primary benefit is that your body can rest and generate more oxygen carrying red blood cells since the oxygen level is higher at a lower Elevation. This will provide you with added strength for the Summit Week.

You will also rest, recover and strengthen your body and mind. You will put on weight and enjoy good food. You will also be able to get on the Internet very easily, anytime, anywhere.

The psychological benefits are equally compelling. You will feel very happy and relaxed. Your motivation level will be high and you will be ready to attempt the Summit Push.

How far down the Valley to go?
You should at least go to Pheriche (about 7-hour descent from BC) and ideally further down. Pheriche will become rather boring after a couple of days. Similarly Tengboche with its Monastry and cake shop.

The best place is certainly Namche Bazar, however, this is further down the valley and you need to return to BC. The real downside of Namche is that you get so comfortable that you don't wish to return to BC for the Summit Attempt!

Ideally, you could Helicopter two-way to Namche which would take 15 minutes rather than 2 days each way. If you cant budget for two-way Heli, then strongly recommend Heli from Namche back to BC. A further option is to spen a night at Pheriche and Heli from Pheriche to Namche. None of our team felt any ill effects from arriving by Heli to BC from Namche.

At Namche, you can stay in a Lodge with Private Shower of USD15 per night. You should budget minimum USD20 per day for F&B expenses.

How long and when to return to BC?
This will be largely dependent on the date you finish your final Acclimatisation Rotation and the Summit Weather Window opening for the Summit Push

It is likely a minimum 5 days down Valley from BC and more likely longer. This is a further reason to consider two-way Heli or at least one-way back to BC. You will and should keep in contact with your Leadership in BC for updates.

Week 7 - Summit Push
Expedition Resource Strategy
At BC ask the question What are the Sherpa Resources available for the Summit Push on the Summit Night? Specifically, if its 1-1 ratio, is there a back-up "Sherpa Reserve" either going for the Summit or in C4?

For example, if someone is in difficulty and needs to descend to C4, this may require 2 no. Sherpas. Is there extra Sherpas available or does it mean a Member must wait-out on the mountain or what?

Will you be split into sub-teams? What is the "order of march" on the Summit night or spread over 2 or more days?

Will you be given a second attempt at the Summit, if you cannot success the first time?

On what basis is this determined? For example the weather may be bad or you are too tired. The weather may improve or you may still find the motivation and energy to try again, noting you will likely be exhausted and depleted your Oxygen and personal food/drink.

The Weather
This is one of the most critical factors in determining whether you will succeed, ascend/descend the Mountain and risk to yourself. Mountain Weather is variable, and Mt Everest can create its own weather system.

How will your Expedition get the Weather Report and Green Light to Go? Your Team Leadership may have Weather Report from an "expert" overseas.

However, the reality is relatively simple, look outside your tent at what is happening on the Mountain, look what the other Expeditions are doing, is the "line of ants" moving up the mountain?, talk to the other Expeditions. Your Leadership and Sherpas will take care of this.

The other reality is that Summit Week is around the same time each year, 3rd week of May, sometimes shorter or longer. Equally, sometimes there is more then one Summit-window.

When is best to leave BC for Summit Push?
There is a Summit Window which may last a few days or upto a week, typically. All remaining Climbers on the Mountain will go during this window.

I recommend as late as practically possible. Ask yourself do you want to be one of those ants in a line of hundreds of people going up in a line to the high camps and then to the Summit, and down? This becomes a more critical issue/risk on C4 to the Summit, particularly the final cornice ridge line both ascending and descending this. Note, If you are stationary for any period of time on the Summit night, you will rapidly get very cold and deteriorate. The total number of other Climbers from other expeditions will have a direct impact on your Summit success or otherwise.

Our Team left BC later than others and subsequently we arrived at C4 at almost the end of the Summit Window, certainly very few Climbers left on the mountain and perhaps a handful going for Summit.

When we were at C2, we could see the line of ants moving up the Lhotse Face and traversing across to C4. On our Summit night, from C4 to Summit, there were No Climbers ahead of us. This was both very special to "have the mountain to ourselves" and also reduced the Risk considerably. Arguably, this lower potential Risk from no other Climbers going for the Summit is a very considerable benefit. This lower Risk has multiple benefits:
- Speed is not controlled/restricted by others up or down, including if climbers get into difficulties and cause blockage

- The longer time/exposure you spend going up / down the higher the risk to yourself as a result of altitude, exhaustion, oxygen supply, and weather related risks
- Less risk of someone falling or dislodging rocks/ice.

What time is best to leave C4 for the Summit?
Generally teams leave for the Summit at night, depending what time they target to reach the Summit, it may take around 10 hours, more or less. There is no fixed turnaround time, however, I suggest the following logic:
- you need to be back at C4 before dusk, which is around 18.00
- it takes 4 – 6 hours on average to descend to C4, assuming you have been ascending for upto 10 hours already
- therefore you need to be heading down around 1200 – 1400, regardless of where you are on the mountain.
- Note: this is dependent on the mountain conditions/weather and your personal situation at the time. Adjust accordingly.

You really dont want to spend a second night in the open and particularly descending. You will likely be exhausted already, it will be dark, very cold and you are at higher risk of falling and passing-away. We departed 20.00 and summitted 06.00, returning to C4 mid-morning. This worked perfectly for our team and there is slack in this timing, particularly the arrival time back in C4.

Personal Radio and Satellite Phone - do I need one ?
In my opinion, this is not essential. It adds personal weight and if you have a personal Sherpa they will have a radio (or nearby Team Sherpa). If you feel you want that added "insurance" then ask your Company, in advance before you have signed-up, whether this is an option. Of course, if somehow you are on your own, then both Personal Radio and/or Satellite Phone may help rescue, but you will need to be able to describe precisely your location.

Week 8 - Trek out to Kathmandu
After a celebratory dinner at BC, you may choose to Trek-Out next day or so or consider Helicopter. You dont need to decide until you are back at BC. At this point, you may also be generous and give Tips or leave personal equipment behind as gifts for Porters and so forth.

A Trek will take minimum 3 – 4 days to Lukla. But why rush? Perhaps use it as a chance to decompress and enjoy a quiet Khumbu Valley - you are the last people in the season. Spend a couple of nights in Namche and savor what you have done with your fellow Climbers, Lodge, and Restaurant Owners that you will have come to know. Enjoy a pizza, curry, burger, momos, capuchino, and chocolate cake

We opted for Heli. A Heli will take less than an hour and take you to Kathmandu directly (so that you can be in Thamel for beers and pizza). We trekked-out to Pheriche in one day and then opted for Heli to Namche. You can equally spend a couple of nights in Namche enroute, as we did. Note, it is likely you will spend a minimum 5 days in Kathmandu upon arrival, assuming Duffles are not on Heli with you. How will you spend your time I wonder !?. A Heli will cost approximately USD3,000, or USD 700 per person. However, your 2 x Duffles will likely be Portered-out to Lukla and put on a plane. There is a real possibility that they get delayed in Lukla, due to bad weather, as was the case with our duffles, which will result in more R&R time in Kathmandu!

15. The Route – beyond Base Camp to the Summit and Return

This is it! You have now been 6 weeks on the Mountain. All things being equal, you have a reasonable chance of attempting the Summit. Well done! Below is an example Route Plan, however this obviously depends on the specific situation at the time and needs to be adjusted accordingly.

The climbing can be broken down into the following phases and summarised as follows:
1. Ice Fall
2. Western Cwm
3. Lhotse Face
4. Lhotse Face to South Col
5. The Summit (South East Ridge)
6. The Return

The Summit night can be broken down further, for example, C4 to Balcony, Balcony to South Summit, and finally South Summit to true Summit. As I have said previously, this enables you to break the mountain into chunks and goals so that you can focus on the immediate task or goal and "eat the elephant a piece at a time". Do not think too far ahead and focus on whats immediately ahead of you and today – the next step is whats important.

Route	Average Time Estimate (hours)
BC to C1	8+
C1 to C2	4+
C2 to C3	8+
C3 to C4	8+
C4 to Summit	10+
Summit to C4	5+
C4 to C2	8+
C2 to BC	5+

C2 looking towards the Lhotse Face
19/05/2018

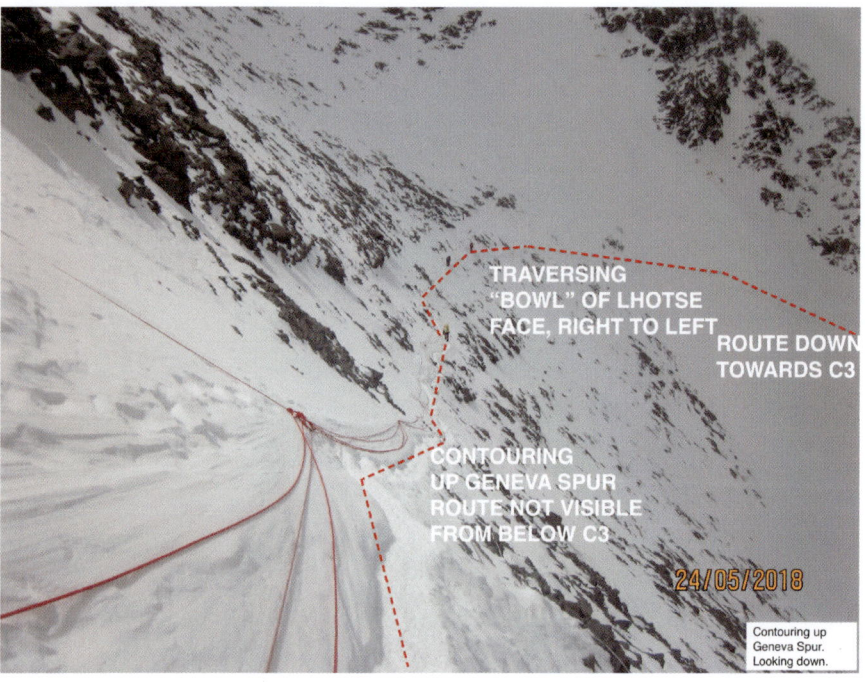

Contouring up Geneva Spur. Looking down.
24/05/2018

Photo 1 labels:
- BALCONY 8443m
- VERY STEEP FACE - about 400m
- GRADUAL INCLINE SLOPE
- FROM C4 8000m
- FINAL SECTION OVER GENEVA SPUR
- 21/05/2018
- Top Geneva Spur

Photo 2 labels:
- South Summit (True Summit not visible)
- Balcony
- Steep Face
- View of Face from C4 N.B. Cannot see True Summit

True
Summit
Mt Everest
South
Summit
Cornice
knife-Edge
Ridge
Line
South East Ridge to Summit
Balcony further down,
bottom right
View from Lhotse
To
Balcony

23/05/2018

Near Summit
Cornice Ridge Line

BC to Camp 1 thru Ice Fall (C1 approximately 6200m+)
The Ice Fall deserves your full Respect, always. You need to move quicky, efficiently and safely. Pay attention and be observant to your surroundings, your foot placement, and whats underneath. Be careful also of whats above, both ice-towers and any freshly placed rocks, that likely have fallen from high above i.e. the "popcorn field".

The Icefall is a jumbled mass of ice-blocks, ice towers, and crevasses, that are shifting and moving downwards to the Khumbu Valley below. It is also prone to avalanches and rocks falling from the shoulder of Mt Everest above and lesser extent Nuptse. The Ice Fall changes year-to-year and in fact, will change over the 2 months you are there, not completely but different sections, resulting in modification to the route, ladders, ropes and so forth.

You will feel apprehensive and fear, this is good and normal especially the first time. The Ice Fall presents the first major pyscological fear factor. It reduces subsequent rotations, but the risk hasn't actually changed, rather your internal comfort level has! Be Careful, don't become complacent. You will wake up early o'clock, maybe 11 pm (or later) and start to get organized in the cold, dark of your tent. You will have something to eat in the dining tent and get your gear on. This anticipation and getting ready, may be as stressful as going thru the Ice Fall itself, so dont be alarmed – it's normal, it shows your mind understands the risk!

1. I will start with my personal experience the first time I went thru the Ice Fall in 2017 and lesson to learn
    a. It was about 0200. A Sherpa from different team tapped me on the shoulder and pointed to my boot. My Crampon was coming off, however not only was my crampon detaching but the entire Heel of my 8000m boot. My immediate thought was one of shock, fear and "my expedition is over". However, as luck and good-skills would have it, a fellow member was carrying some very robust extra Mountain boot lace and he was directly behind me (who brings string with them!). In addition one of our Sherpas happened to be next to me. The Sherpa effected a repair in the middle of the Ice Fall and I successfully albeit gingerly made it to C1. In fact, both boots failed. A couple of days later the black masking tape arrived from Base Camp and the crampons on both boots were permanently taped to the Boots. This is how they remained for the entire Training Climb Expedition to Camp 3 and back, safely. An interesting side observation is that it's not entirely necessary to remove Crampons each day (but you should check they are fitted securely. This saves time/energy.
2. Timings
    a. The first time may take 8 - 10 hours and serious elevation gain from about 5375m to 6200m. Think about that. You have read in the books that 300m is typically "safe" daily elevation gain. You will be exhausted like you have never felt before.
    b. Crampon Point. When you leave your tent after having a breakfast you will walk thru BC and into the Ice Fall to a place called Crampon Point. At this point you will stop and put your crampons on.
    c. I recommend leaving BC around midnight, rather than later say 02.00. Why?
        i. If you leave 0200 then around 0800 as you exit the Ice Fall you will be walking in the bright, burning sun for say several hours, say 3+ hours and arrive at about mid-day.

        ii. If you leave midnight, you will reduce your exposure to walking in the burning Sun and arrive say 1000. Ideally, you need to arrive at C1 as the sun rises.
        iii. This time in the Sun will destroy you. It will take longer to recover and put serious doubts in your mind. You will come to a grinding halt
        iv. The Sun will reflect of the glaring white Ice Fall and Glacier around you and the sides of Everest and Nuptse, so you will be cooked from all directions, hence the name "Western BBQ".
        v. Be ready to talk off your layers to only your top base layer. In the middle-east in desert type terrains the local clothing is typically white, and for a good reason. Common sense would say white reflects better than black color base Layer (most people wear black/darker colors for some reason). Your Leg Shell should have zips so you can ventilation to your legs
- d. As daylight approaches, you feel and see that you are thru most of the Ice Fall and sense the Western Cym opening in front of you and the sides of Everest and Lhotse more visible. Be careful, don't be too happy, it's not over, there is a long way to go to get to C1. Yes, you have finished the Ice Fall and are feeling very happy with yourself but it is now a series of winding switch-backs, and very exhausting ups and downs at the bottom of the Glacier as it "falls" into what becomes the Ice Fall.
- e. You see yellow Tents in distance, but which is your Camp. The Camps are spread out in the area that is C1. It is like a "mirage" and you seem to keep going without arriving at your Camp and by now you are desperate.
- f. Take it easy, don't blow yourself up and try to rush to C1 whilst feeling completely exhausted. Stop, drink, enjoy the accomplishment and the view.
- g. It is in this "morning cooking time" where you are the "sausage being fried" in the "Western BBQ" that you will desperately appreciate a cold 1 liter of electrolyte drink, so think about that when packing at BC. You leave in the dark and you don't think you will be drinking much but in fact, you will be desperate for a drink in the daylight hours.
- h. Inside your C1 tent, the temperature may rise to plus 40c and you will both cook and go "berserk". Equally, it is difficult to sit outside, due to often cold breeze. I strongly recommend your team brings a tarpaulin that connects between the tents to shelter you from the sun and enable group members to sit outside whilst avoiding the sun.

2. The Ropes thru the Ice Fall
    a. Always clip-in with your safety line,
    b. use Jumar as appropriate
    c. Accidents and slips happen when we don't expect them and falling here may be very bad
    d. Avoid having any time-period when you are not attached or at least holding onto the line i.e. when clipping carabiner to next section of rope

3. Ladders thru the Ice Fall

a. Ladders are like Parachuting. In parachuting its generally not jumping out of the plane that kills you, rather hitting the gound. Similarly, its easy to cross the ladders, if you stay calm.
b. You can practice at home but it's not quite the same staring down a 100ft crevasse.
c. You may also be given an opportunity at BC, closer to reality, however you will quickly adjust to learning how to traverse the ladders.
d. Ladders are in all orientations and lengths. Horizontal, declining, inclining, even angled to the side. It's about Balance. Some ladder sections or gaps may be up to 5 no. 12ft ladders joined together, this means crossing a rather big crevasse and the ladder will naturally bow and bounce in the middle
e. There may be 10 - 20 ladder sections in total thru the Ice Fall, perhaps more. It depends on the year.
f. Check is my Harness secure above hips (this is important)? My harness has previously fallen around my legs (perhaps since I had lost weight. Worst case you fall, the harness is what will hopefully save you.
g. This is my technique for when you face the ladders and about to step-off - go into "Zombie Mode":
   i. Take 3 breathes
   ii. Clear your Mind, become Zen-Calm
   iii. Clip-in and hold the ropes. Make sure ropes are taught, either yourself or with your climbing buddies.
   iv. Focus on the Crampon front-points and position them on the first rung of the ladder and lower your boot correctly. Feel that it's secure. Repeat other boot. I don't recommend putting the middle of your boot on the rung, less stable, less bite.
   v. You cannot avoid looking down. Embrace it.
   vi. Repeat
h. The Guide Lines are that, guide lines only. Keep them taught and with tension, whichever the orientation of the Ladders, it will vary.
i. Use your buddy or Sherpa to put their foot at either end of the ladder, if two people and tension the line. This will become standard practice.

Camp 1 in the Western Cym or valley is an awe inspiring place and you are surrounded by the Mountain Gods, west ridge of Everest to your left, Lhotse face directly in front and the north face of Nuptse to the right (ohh, and thankfully the Ice Fall behind you!). Note at C1 it is unlikely you will have a Dining Tent.

You feel exhausted, satisfied, more like relief that you have made it thru the Ice Fall and a well-deserved rest from the total feeling of exhaustion. This type of exhaustion you may not have experienced before in your life and does not compare with other strenuous physical activities at Sea Level. Your body feels like a "flat battery". Remember you have made a large elevation gain in a relatively short period, from 5375m to 6200m, where you will sleep. Rest, Rehydrate, Recover. Tomorrow you will hopefully feel better.

Ice Fall Ladder across Crevasse

C1 to C2 (C2 approximately 6400m+)
The route to C2 looks relatively flat and short and you can almost identify the general C2 location in the distance from C1, to the left of the glacier, base of Mt Everest's shoulder.

This seemingly gentle slope route to C2 will have many switch-backs like a maze soon after C1, very large crevasses that will likely necessitate multiple ladders joined together, some steep but relatively safe vertical up and down climbs thru the crevasses in the glacier and then become a straight long trail direct to C2. Many of these crevasses that you are required to vertically ascend or abseil down are very different to the ice-fall and appear relatively "safer" and larger. You will be able to see the C2 Tents get larger.

As you start from C1 be ready for the exhaustion to hit you. You will be like an ant under a magnifying glass, the sun from above and reflected from all around you. Ideal weather is overcast with a gentle breeze. You are likely to only be able to walk a few steps and stop and rest. You may end up on your knees, as I have seen people do. I have known several incredibly physically fit people whom have reached their end and quit the Expedition at this point. Perhaps the extreme exhaustion, mental doubts coupled with the confusion "Why am I so weak when the trail is so seemingly flat and easy ?". Again, simply remember the basics, go slowly, stop, rest and go at a pace that is comfortable for you, not others. There is no rush to arrive at C2. It is most important that you arrive at C2, rather then forced to quit or return to C1. It is perhaps a 4-hour walk only.

Note C2 camps are stretched out over approximately 200m+ distance going towards Lhotse, depending your Expedition Company C2 location.

At C2 it is very likely you will have a Dining Tent and the environment is more comfortable then C1.

C1 to C2
Crevasses
Western Cwm

Climbing
between C1 and C2
Western Cwm

Abseiling
Between C1 & C2
Western Cwm

C2 to C3 (C3 approximately 7200m)

This is a Big Day Out.

From C2 it is still a 1 to 2 hours hike to the base of the Lhotse Face and end of the Cwm. This is not technically difficult and no major risks or challenges although it is on a shallow, gradual incline which will still sap your energy. This will be an exhausting hike as you stare constantly at the looming Lhotse Face that you have seen from the first day after arriving at Base Camp.

At the base of the Face, I felt a Cosmic energy feeling, the triangulation of Everest, Nuptse, and Lhotse. Almost a feeling of Levitation - which would have been great !.

The Lhotse Face is impressive and looming. You will say to yourself it looks massive and steep. The truth is once you come face to face and "kiss the face" you will be surprised that maybe it's not as bad as you imagined and not as seemingly vertical! This principle of "kissing the face" applies to all aspects of the mountain

The most dangerous part of the Lhotse Face is arguably here at the bottom - take care and move efficiently (do not hang-around here), pay attention to above and eyes and ears open. Let's consider:
- You will rest about 50m before the bottom of the face, in a relatively safe location
- You may cross a ladder across a Bergstrund at the base of the Face. Next, using ropes and Jumar, maybe ascend a short, steep section and now properly go up the Face. In 2017 this was a mini Ice Cliff, however in 2018, this was less technical and less steep.
- This point on the face is effectively like a funnel where rocks, debris, 1-Litre bottles, and larger Thermos flasks will come rocketing down. I have also seen an Oxygen Bottle fly past like a torpedo. These have the potential to either seriously injure you or worse. As you ascend on the Line the first, relatively steep 50m you will have a very restricted view of what's above and cannot see much of the Face above. You need to not delay here and move expeditiously.
- Once you are out of this immediate Funnel-zone you will see the long line of climbers up ahead of you going up the Face. There is still a very real risk of falling objects from above all the way until you arrive at your C3. You will often hear people shout "rock" and you will need to quickly decide which way to move, left or right.
- There are a few very short steeper sections of mixed rock/ice that you will clamber over and become a bottleneck. Certainly not a technical challenge, just physical effort.

It is a hard, steep slog that never seems to end to reach C3. It's not technically difficult, rather more physically and mentally demanding. You may feel pain in your Achilles due to the steep angle of the face, however you are effectively still walking upwards like a penguin i.e. no real "front-pointing". You will use the Jumar but remember your arms and upper body are weak muscles compared to your legs, which should be doing the real work – technique. Your motivation and ability to keep going will be severly tested, your ability to simply put one foot in front of the other is the key. You will ask yourself "where is C3", "are we nearly there yet". Try to focus on a short term mini-goal say 100m above you and then the next mini-goal. It is very important that when you reach each anchor point you do the basics right, and connect your safety caribiner to the upper side of the anchor before detaching your Jumar. It will also be important to ensure your mitts/gloves are tied around your wrists.

The different Expedition Company Camp 3 locations are spread out, sometimes over 1-200 meters vertically on the face. If you leave C3 dont be complacent, make sure you clip-in - if you slip and slide you will not stop, until the bottom.

Tip: you will have your 8000m sleeping bag and 8000m down suit in your backpack, however may not be wearing the 8000m suit yet. You may consider just stuffing into your backpack rather then to expend energy and try packing in their respective stuff-bags. This applies elsewhere on route too.

C3 to C4 (C4 at 8000m)
This is another Big Day-Out
Probably the night before or in the morning you will now be on Oxygen until you Summit and return to C3 i.e. upto 5 days. This will help you greatly and give you that extra boost. If you made it this far and barring any medical or weather situations you should be in with a good shot at a Summit Attempt, standing on the Summit hopefully in only 24 hours from now!

What to wear? This depends on the weather conditions and how hot or cold you feel – the layer principle applies. Myself I was wearing base-layer (top and bottom), fleece and Goretex jacket. I wore my cap under my helmet and wore my glacier glasses. If needed I could put on my mid layer puffer jacket, beanie or even 8000m suit if really needed (although unlikely). I was wearing my liner gloves and mitts as required.

Ascending upwards from C3
Do not imagine that your C3 is the "top" of the Lhotse Face and no more ascending, just a traverse across the Face, this is very wrong. On leaving C3 there is a further steep ascent up the Lhotse Face before reaching a point where you will make a near 90 degree left turn and traverse across the Face, like a bowl around and upwards, crossing the Yellow Band to the Geneva Spur and up and over it to C4. You will not leave C3 until after daylight, perhaps 730am or later, due to the cold and preferably when the Sun's rays hit C3.

Traverse across the Face. This traverse is less physically demanding compared to when you leave C3 to reach the turning point. As always ensure you are clipped-in on this traverse across the Face, else it is a very long slide down to the bottom and certain death. There is a well worn, visible albeit narrow snow path that follows the rope line that you will use. People may overtake you or go past you coming down the path. Lean into the path if people are passing you on the way down (or up).

Yellow Band. As you ascend there will be sections of rock that are yellow-ish in color, hence the name. These do not pose any real technical difficulty or risk, however, I strongly advise you have careful   foot placement, despite wearing your crampons, on these rocks on the ascent and especially the descent since they will likely slip. Myself, I slipped about 15 ft on the descent due to poor foot placement skills manouevering one particular section of Yellow-band rocks. I was of course on the rope and managed to arrest my fall quickly and clamber, front-point back across to the path, unscathed, except for the shock to the system.

Geneva Spur. You will be relieved to not be ascending upwards compared to the section after leaving C3 and after traversing across the bowl Face you go up a gradual incline path that contours the Spur on the Everest side of the Lhotse Face. This route does not pose any real technical difficulty or risk, unless hit from above or not clipped-in and fall. Note, you cannot see this last section of the route behind the Geneva Spur from the Western Cym, only from C3 onwards. You will then ascend a steep, near vertical 25m+ section of mixed terrain to almost the same elevation as the South Col, 8000m. This is not technically difficult, you will be on a Jumar and good foot placement options, either kicked-in ice steps or rocky sections (more caution is needed on the climb-down).

Note, as you ascend to C4, traverse the Face and near the Geneva Spur, the views are very special looking down the Face, the yellow-band below you on Nuptse and the Valley far below now. Take time to stop, and savor the view, you are well above the clouds of the Khumbu Valley far below.

Arrival into C4, South Col, 8000m - WOW !

You should aim to arrive at C4 late afternoon, around 3pm+. You are now at the top of the Geneva Spur and a gentle, near horizontal 100m hike largely over granite slabs into C4. You will round the top of the Geneva Spur and for the first time see the final Summit Night Route to the Top (you cannot see the actual Summit). WOW! Seeing the view of the final route for the first time on the Expedition was awe inspiring and I felt like a real Adrenalin rush.

C3 looking upwards towards top-left Yellow Band

Ascending from C3 towards Yellow Band
Left turn approaching

21/05/2018

Yellow Band
Geneva Spur
Mt Everest Face

21/05/2018

Crossing the
Yellow Band
towards C4

21/05/2018

Geneva Spur in foreground Everest S.East Ridge in background

24/05/2018

Final steep section up & over Geneva Spur behind

Top Geneva Spur.
C4 Tents. Left is
"ramp" up Everest

21/05/2018

C4
South Col

Camp 4 to the Summit 8848m and down to C4 – a two-way trip
Typically you will be resting for a few hours from when you arrive at C4 to departing C4 for your Summit Attempt, although this depends on various factors and you may spend a night at C4. For example, you may arrive about 4 pm and depart between 8 pm – 10 pm, depending on your Team readiness, leadership decision, and the weather.

This will be a long 24 hours of mostly hard work at maximum altitude with little rest or sleep. Think about it. It seems incredibly tough but once you are at this point in the Expedition you will find the extra energy reserves, adrenalin and perhaps excitement that you are now less then 24 hours from reaching the Summit!

You need to appreciate:
- this will probably be the most exhausting and risky 15+ hours of the entire Expedition. It is really steep and therefore the descent is particularly risky and demanding on the legs and needs your full concentration.
- Two of the key variables and risks are not in your Control i.e. the weather and other climbers. You may find yourself in a helpless situation, in bad-weather, high-winds, freezing temperatures and stuck in a bottle-neck behind other climbers. If you find yourself alone, woken from sleep, the wind in your face then do not be troubled, you may be dead or close to death and its upto you to summon yourself to your feet or lie down.

The Approximate timings are:
1. C3 to C4   8 hours
2. C4 to Summit   10 hours
3. Summit to C4   4 - 6 hours
   TOTAL   24 hours

I arrived about 4 pm at C4 with the Head Sherpa, who was also double-timing as my Personal Sherpa. Whilst inside the tent I was preparing to depart for Summit at about 8pm the same day. In those few hours in I did the following:
- ate my crisp tube,
- ate half a packet of figs,
- ate a chocolate bar
- drank a 500ml bottle of fizzy/coffee drink (one of two that I prepared in BC for the Summit Night).
- Did a "No.2" toilet (whilst using my Oxygen)
- Popped 2 no. anti-diarrhea pills. I have previously relieved myself at 7,000m+ on a steep incline on another Mountain and do not wish to repeat the experience on Mt Everest at 8,000m+. I cannot imagine anything worse then wearing a Summit Suit, using Oxgen and on a steep incline trying to relieve oneself and then clean-up afterwards!

In addition, drank a liter of water and noodles prepared by the Sherpas. Therefore I was very carbo-loaded and ready for the 8pm call to Action. Note, you may burn upto 20,000 calories on the Summit-push. However things didnt go to Plan. My other team members arrived and the Leadership decided that we should not depart for the Summit this night since in-sufficient rest and recovery and Summit attempt would therefore be less likely to be successful. Therefore we would go for the Summit in 24 hours and stay an extra night at the "C4 Death Zone Holiday Beach Club", a bit like the rocky Brighton beach in England, however unfortunately I did not bring my deck-chair, newspaper and handerchief to wrap around my head (and no fish n chips either!).   Our Summit attempt was now in the hands of the Mountain Gods and the Weather, which could change at any moment, thereby jeopardizing the last 2 months. This is not normally understood practice, however, flexibility is required to assess the situation at a given point in time and consider the needs of the Group in totality, rather than the needs of the individual i.e. myself. Could I have gone with my Sherpa for the Summit? In theory Yes, but in reality No. This would have increased the risks to ourselves with only two of us on the Summit Attempt, particuarlly if something went wrong. Also, it is a Group Expedition, not a solo expedition with a Sherpa. Thankfully the next evening the weather was good and we departed about 8pm.

<u>When the "green light" comes on and the Leader/Sherpa tells you, get a grip and GO! Dont delay, dont flinch, dont loose "your bottle" now.</u>

Approximate durations based on our 10 hour Ascent from C4 to Summit
- C4 to Balcony: 4 – 6 hours
- Balcony to South Summit: 3 - 5 hours
- South Summit to True Summit: 1 - 2 hours

1. You will depart your tent at night. This is it, but try to calm yourself.
2. What to wear and bring? It will be cold in your tent. You will likely be leaving C4 wearing your base layers, fleece, down puffer jacket underneath your Down Suit. You may rapidly burn-up and should stop and remove at least your puffer jacket, probably before you start on the steep face ascent, which I did.
    a. Do your gear check however the major items you will be familiar with and not likely to forget to wear, including torch, beany and so forth

- b. Bring spare torch battery, high-altitude medicines, throat lozenges, sun-cream, possibly spare mitts.
- c. It will be dark when you depart C4 but do <u>not</u> forget your Glacier Glasses and Ski Goggles, especially for the descent in daylight, else game-over! On the Ascent you may choose not to wear depending the weather, although it can get very cold, especially with even a slight wind.
- d. I carried my 500ml fizzy drink inside my down suit jacket (which I made sure was "flat" at BC) blended with quadruple expresso that I made in Base Camp a week ago. I should add that my Mask froze to my face, with icicles and ice and was painful to remove and have a drink. Minimum 2 no.
- e. Bring Gels with maximum Caffeine content – you will get tired going thru the night. It's no different to walking thru the night anythwere in the world, you will feel tired. Minimum 6 no.
- f. Bring chocolate/energy bars. Minimum 4 no.
- g. Optional: 1-litre drink in your day-pack or possibly down suit inner pocket. There is high-probability that will freeze, even if put within your down booty. This becomes a 1kg weight. It may thaw in the morning. If you can manage to keep a bottle close to your body, inside your jacket, this is the only way to avoid freezing. However in the morning it may have melted to enable you to drink, hopefully at the Balcony.
- h. Bring spare batteries for your torch, unless you have a powerful torch with a multi-battery pack that can be put in your down suit jacket pocket (this is what I used).
- i. Note: the extra food/gels you can put in your day-pack and as you eat the supply contained within the inner pocket of your down jacket you can replace and warm them up gradually.

3. Walk across the rocky, flat, South Col about 100m towards the face. Be careful of your foot placement thru the rocks in the dark – you dont want to fall and twist your ankle here.
4. You are now directly in front of the looming dark Mt Everest Face and will gradually move up an incline slope to the base of the face (minimal risk here). Go slowly, dont blow-up, calm yourself, remove extra layers of clothing if too hot (I removed by inner puffer-jacket so that I had my base-layer, fleece and Summit suit remaining). You will see the head torches of your team mates high above you, on the face. Amazing.
5. You will move up a gradual packed snow ramp that will become steeper after 100m.
6. You are at the base of the Face. The face will now get very steep suddenly and continue upwards relentlesly, an ascent of approximately 400m to the Balcony. This is it. You will be using your Jumar continously now. It's not technically difficult or risky, unless you are not always attached to the line, but very hard work that seems to never end. There are anchor points and you will switch over the anchor points per normal routine. This slope is perhaps similar or in fact harder than the Lhotse Face. The angle is steep and your achilles may burn as you mostly penguin step. If you were to see the ridge line to the Balcony from Lhotse (refer Route picture) you would be "impressed" by the drop either side, however it will be dark so no concern
    - a. If you are knackered at any point on the ascent talk to Sherpa and consider increasing your oxygen flow. This is important, it will help you get thru a difficult time and help you stabilize and recover. You can obviously turn-down the flow-rate depending how you feel. Your Sherpa will suggest the appropriate setting for you based on experience.

- b. You will make a right turn into the Balcony (approximately 8443m) which has enough area for you all to stand comfortably. At Balcony, change Oxygen, eat, drink, rest, re-group, focus – you are only 400m from the Summit!. Look at the head torches of your team mates on the Lhotse Couloir also – you are the same elevation as their Summit - very special.
- c. Continue upwards, climbing ice/snow/rocky terrain and some rocky step sections, along the ridge to South Summit (approximately 8748m). These rocky sections may surprise you but you will clamber up and over them – go slowly, no rush – they wont stop you, step-by-step, no rush. The Sun will rise to your right side over Tibet, maybe 0400, by now you are approaching the Summit. You are making good progress and the Sunrise is always a mental boost, especially on this day and this special place.
- d. Note, there is about a 30ft rock wall near the South Summit which you will assault in the dark, and that presents a small challenge. Its a matter of taking it slowly and foot placement. Frankly speaking, you will get up and over it, whatever it takes no doubt, it's not going to stop you, if you are this close to the Summit, is it?! Drive-on, one step in front of another. There are also various smaller mixed rock/ice sections that you need to climb over also.

7. Cornice Ridge Line to Summit. From the South Summit at 8748m you will traverse approximately the last 100m of elevation along a knife-edge corniced ridge to the true Summit at 8848m. A large part, not all, of the final 100m elevation will be on the ridge line however close to the Summit becomes more of a wider, flatter, inclined, open-path. This ridge-line is one of the hardest and most riskiest sections of the entire Mountain. This may surprise you when you see it, give you some fear and another reason to avoid many people on the route.
- a. This will be intimidating and the Mountain has provided a final hard test directly prior to your arrival at the Summit, the flags you can see in the distance. It's not necessarily technically difficult but you need to take care.
- b. It's a clear, roped route, in many places a very narrow route, that undulates up and down and requires you to clamber over and around obstacles (hard-packed snow, rock, ice and the former Hillary Step). On your right is South West Face (Tibet) and left is the sheer drop of the Kangshung Face (Nepal). However, the challenge/risk is really on the descent down this ridge line.
- c. The drop either side is a long way down, perhaps 3 km or more each side of the ridge or the "Grand Tour" rapid descent option. The cornice is on your right shoulder and difficult to imagine falling off into Tibet side. Worst case, you are very unlikely to fall 3km unless you are not clipped-in or somehow other low-probability events like rope breaks. If you do fall any distance you are likely at the very least to be banged-up badly, since rocky, so dont think "its ok, I am clipped-in, even if I do fall".
- d. As you near the True Summit it becomes a snow slope, widens and the angle seems less steep.

8. Summit. Relief and Satisfaction in equal measure. Ideally, you should aim to summit in the morning, perhaps around 0600. Do what you need to do and expeditiously get down safely to C4 – dont spend too long here, the variables can change quickly and risk increase sharply i.e. bad weather, bottle-necks, altitutude illness, snow blindness.

9. Summit descent to C4. The Sun is hopefully shining and it's a great feeling, although you are exhausted. The ridgeline descent is arguably the riskiest place on the Summit section and you need to take great care. Stay close to your Sherpa. Remember that you are likely to feel:
    a. elated
    b. exhausted
    c. suffering, perhaps from lack of Oxygen
    d. not thinking clearly
    e. paying less attention
    f. and the forces of gravity apply, your Jumar does not work on the descent and there is increased risk of falling some distance, even though clipped in with your caribiner.
10. Descend cautiously to Balcony. Once at Balcony take a proper rest and recover. You are close to C4 and can clearly see C4 Tents.
11. Remember, the Balcony to C4 is just as steep a descent as the ascent however now you dont have your Jumar working and the forces of gravity, so there is an increased risk of falling on this steep face. By now you will be very exhausted also albeit happy. Stay mentally focussed and find the energy for this last part into C4.

Mt Everest Summit Looking towards Tibet

Descent - Camp 4 to C2

The next day. This can be done in a day with arrival around 5 pm at C2 as the sun sets down the valley. I recommend that you descend to C2, stopping briefly at C3 to rest and collect any stashed personal gear, all factors permitting. It is unusual to stay at C3 on the descent and the lower elevation of C2 will be much more preferable then C3

For our team, the weather started to change, and the weather window was effectively closing, perhaps we summitted on the last day of the season and I am not aware of others summitting in the days after ourselves.

Whilst descending thru the yellow-band, be careful of your foot placement and preferably not place them on the rocks, rather in between!.

For myself and Tent-Buddy, as we descended the Lhotse Face, it was impossible to clip into the line to try a proper repell or any abseil on certain sections, since the rope was wet and heavy. Instead we simply forward hand-rapped almost the entire face, including backward repelling with a hand-grip at the steeper, bottom section of the face. This was fine, perhaps we were more confident but there was no real alternative.

Note, you may be very exhausted and the cumulative effect of the last few days may finally hit you when you arrive at C2. You may feel sick, not be able to sleep and very cold in your sleeping bag. Several of our team suffered in this way and myself, I felt very cold in my sleeping bag at C2 regardless of what I tried to do to warm-up. Dont be surprised.

C4 descending to C3. Looking down the steep Face

Descending from C3 in white-out conditions

Descent - C2 to BC
This is it, the final section of your Summit Week to the relative safety and comfort of BC.

Remember, the Ice Fall remains treacherous, again do not be complacent and you are not "safe" until you arrive at BC, where you can breathe a sigh of relief and finally relax.

You will notice that the Ice Fall is changing and melting, particularly the lower sections near BC with fast glacial streams flowing. It was April, late Spring when you arrived and now nearly June, the start of the summer. It's been a long long Trip.

I departed C2 about 0730 and arrived at BC about 1230pm, in time for Lunch. You will walk thru your former C1 which is not likley to exist anymore. This is a feeling of pure relief and happiness. Your only major task is packing your duffles and making the choice of whether to trek-out or take a Helicopter, I chose the later direct to Kathmandu and Thamel!

Unfortunately one of our Lhotse team members went into a crevasse in the Ice Fall resulting in a broken ankle. He made it to BC and had a Heli Rescue the next day to Kathmandu. A hero.

C4 descending to C3. Looking down the steep Face

Michael and Tenji Sherpa Descending to C2

16. The End – the "Job is done"

The "Job is done". Well done. You did it. Now, move on - to the Next.

Yes, you are on a High. Enjoy it, savor it, celebrate it, extend it before you come back down to Earth - but not for too long. Enjoy the back-slapping in Base Camp, the Pizza in Namche, the Beers in Thamel. You have done a very selfish thing, yes people will want to hear from you but don't let it consume you and make you become too arrogant - come back to Earth from the Top of the World!. Some people say it can take Years to really appreciate that you Summitted Mt Everest, the highest place on Earth, the place you have read about and watched at the Movies. It will rightly decay over time, you will have those "snap-shot memories" and perhaps it is not healthy to be consumed by the mountain which is in reality, a large, old piece of rock, ice, and snow where courageous people have lost their lives.

And if you Failed. Chin-Up. It's part of the long-term process, don't view it too negatively. You are reading this so that's good news. It is certainly "better to have tried and failed then failed to try". Ask Why did you Fail? Didnt put the Time in, Confidence, Emotion, Skill, Fitness, Resouces, Medical, Weather – all of the above? Be honest, maybe ask others opinion and most importantly what are the take-aways for next time. Ask yourself honestly, "How badly do I want to Summit?". If you really want it, you will come back and look at this as part of the training experience, which it is. Learn from your failure, motivate yourself to do better next time.

We all make excuses for our failure. "The weather was bad", "I didn't acclimatise properly", "I have a cold and cough", "I miss home (!)". If its due to the mountain conditions then fair enough, its about keeping alive to come back and fight another day, whilst also noting others may not have quit even though you did - we all have different Limits, which is important to recognise. The Mountain will always be there and you can always come back. However ask yourself honestly, was it down to your own internal weakness? Dig deeper into yourself for the reasons. If so, most importantly, What are you going to change the next time?

Many Summits I have not summited for different reasons, some personal weakness, some to do with external factors. I never felt put-off or decided "that's it, I quit mountaineering", its part and parcel of what comes with Mountaineering, I accept this, calmly and knowingly. There is "no strength without struggle". If your journey was easy it would not be worth it, be less satisfying and not so memorable. It is those hard experiences on a mountain, the cold, the pain, the suffering, yes, those failures, those images, are burned into our minds, that makes us stronger and better prepared for the next time, that brings us back for more. Without pushing beyond your limit and without "sliding down the face" once or twice you will never know what you could have achieved – come back for more. Most importantly is to avoid having a really bad experience that may result in you losing heart, losing the passion and worse, stop mountaineering altogether. If you failed to summit but did it in good grace and style with maximum Effort then perhaps its less important to have summitted then the time spent and experience of getting there. It would arguably be more rewarding to have tried several times and then achieve the summit. Mountaineering is a long-term hobby, a cumulative activity over years that your body and mind learns and adapts to, it is the cumulation of all those Expeditions and experiences that are built over years, step-by-step, building endurance, resilience, it is not like a running a 4-hour marathon or playing a game of Golf.

Finally, if you need reminding, it has taken a lot of effort, time, money and investment. Properly rest and recover ready for the next expedition. Admit it has taken the direct/in-direct support of your family, friends, and colleagues. Rest your body and mind and do something completely different from mountaineering. Perhaps you should return home and focus on Family and Work (well, for the later, to generate enough cash for the next trip…). Perhaps the most important take-away from Mt Everest is reminding ourselves how insignificant we are, mere Mortals, like dust in the wind.

Acknowledgements

Mum and dad, Nora, and Kyan. My friends. My colleagues.
Dan Mazur for his Forward to this book, his Leadership and Friendship.
Especially Tenji Sherpa and the entire 2018 Mt Everest Nepal Team whom I climbed with.

Disclaimer

Copyright 2018 Michael Tomordy
Text, Images and Photographs copyright Michael Tomordy

All rights reserved. No part of this book may be used or reproduced in any manner whatsoever without written permission from the publisher and copyright holders. Requests should be mailed to Michael Tomordy at michaeltomordy@hotmail.com

The information provided in this book is designed to provide information on the topics covered, including preparation, timeline, personal equipment, and training. It is particularly written for people who would like to undertake high-altitude Mountaineering, including Mt Everest.

You should not undertake any of the training and activities described until you have seen qualified medical professionals and been given a clear bill of health. If you are suffering from any physical or medical condition, you should consult with qualified medical professionals immediately. Do not avoid or disregard professional medical advice or delay in seeking it because of what you have read.

All of the information contained in this book is for informational and educational purposes only. The authors of this book shall have no liability or responsibility to any reader or any third party arising out of any injury or damage incurred as a result of the use of the information provided in this book.

Summit Ridge Line.

Printed in Great Britain
by Amazon